Improving Health through Human Resource Management

Mapping the Territory

Dr Paula Hyde

Dr Ruth Boaden,

Penny Cortvriend

Dr Claire Harris,

Professor Mick Marchington

Dr Sarah Pass

Professor Paul Sparrow

Professor Bonnie Sibbald

University of Manchester

© Chartered Institute of Personnel and Development and
the Department of Health 2006

Research included in this book was sponsored by:
the CIPD
the Department of Health
Healthcare People Management Association

First published 2006

Cover design by Curve
Designed and typeset by Beacon Graphics, Gloucestershire
Printed in Great Britain by Short Run Press, Exeter

British Library Cataloguing in Publication Data:
A catalogue record for this book is available from the British Library

ISBN 1 84398 153 X
ISBN-13 978 1 84398 153 4

Chartered Institute of Personnel and Development
151 The Broadway, Wimbledon, London, SW19 1JQ

Tel.: 020 8612 6200
Website: www.cipd.co.uk

Incorporated by Royal Charter: Registered charity no. 1079797.

Contents

Acknowledgements

The authors would like to acknowledge the support given to this research by all those who participated in the consultation process, helping us to ground our ideas in the reality of the NHS and other sectors.

We also owe a debt of thanks to the administrative team at the Centre for Public Policy and Management, Manchester Business School, particularly Lyndsey Jackson, and to Mike Emmott and Rebecca Clake at the CIPD for their project management support and encouragement.

List of figures and tables

Foreword

Huge changes are taking place in the nature and organisation of services provided by the National Health Service, yet there is increasing recognition that health care delivery relies fundamentally on the capacity and capabilities of the workforce.

This Report contains findings from the first phase of a major research project of which the aim is to explore how human resource management can contribute to improved performance in the NHS. This two-and-a-half-year study is being sponsored by the Department of Health, the Chartered Institute of Personnel and Development and Healthcare People Management Association.

It is not the first piece of research to explore the relationship between the way you manage your human resources and the performance of your organisation. In recent years, for example, CIPD research with the University of Bath has made an important contribution to improving the evidence linking people management to business performance. Studies have also shown correlations between mortality rates and HRM practices.

How and *why* HRM and performance are linked remains worthy of further investigation. There are particular challenges posed in the unique context of the NHS. The NHS is the largest employer in Europe and over half of the people it employs are professionally qualified. What is more, vast numbers of people who are not employed by the NHS play a crucial role in the provision of our health care.

The team from the University of Manchester bring to this challenge expertise from the fields of health care, human resource management and psychology. Such a range of skills and experience means that they are exceptionally well placed to undertake this investigation.

This Report represents the starting point for tackling the core of the project. In 'mapping the territory' it critically examines current perspectives on HRM theories and considers their application and relevance in the NHS. The Report also shares the findings from a rigorous literature review examining the empirical evidence for a link between HRM and organisational performance.

The fact that there is no 'magic bullet' – no single element of HRM that will on its own have a dramatic effect on performance – is unlikely to surprise many readers. More important, in practical terms, is the emphasis the authors place on the importance of background and context when it comes to promoting any element of HRM. Care must be taken when seeking to transfer elements of HRM from other sectors to the NHS.

The Report also comments that the 'system' and 'management' are at times seen to be in conflict with professional interests, and that commitment cannot be assumed from all those who provide services, especially where they are not directly employed. There is a need to balance central initiatives with local freedoms. These are issues which have ramifications that go much wider than the HR function. However, unless people management issues are taken fully into account, national initiatives are likely to be less effective in supporting the delivery of local services. The ability of HR professionals to pursue a strategic agenda linked to business outcomes appears currently to be constrained by a number of factors, including the priority that has had to be given to implementing national initiatives.

At the time of writing, the research team are embarking on the second stage of this project. The focus will be on HRM in action, as the team conduct primary research in a selection of NHS settings. This will include six in-depth case studies of 'high-performing' and 'transformational' NHS Trusts over the course of a year. The CIPD, the Department of Health and HPMA look forward to the development of this research, and will continue to share the findings with practitioners.

Rebecca Clake and **Mike Emmott**
Advisers
Chartered Institute of Personnel and Development

Dean Royles
Head of HR Capacity,
Department of Health

Peter King
Executive Director,
Healthcare People Management Association

Executive Summary

This Report summarises the results from the first phase of a research study designed to explore how human resource management (HRM) can contribute to improved performance within the NHS. It is being carried out by a multidisciplinary team who have been at the forefront of both HRM and health policy research, and who have an extensive understanding of leading-edge HRM in other sectors.

The research involved two analyses of existing academic literature – one of the theories of HRM, and one which provides the results of a semi-systematic review of the empirical literature on the HRM–performance link. The current strategy and performance management system of the NHS has been reviewed. In addition, a series of consultation meetings was held with (primarily) NHS staff to explore views on the link between HRM and performance.

Key messages from this research are that:

◘ The NHS is the largest employer in Europe – a complex organisation, undergoing significant structural change, in which the impact of market forces is being increasingly felt.

◘ Those who work to provide health care, not all of whom are employed by the NHS, do a wide range of types of work, and come from a variety of professional groups.

◘ Formal performance management from a national perspective is relatively new within the NHS. The nature of the performance measures used in the NHS is very different from that of measures used in private sector organisations.

◘ Theory about the HRM–performance relationship can be classified as 'best practice'

(high-commitment), 'best fit' (contingency) and 'resource-based'. Current research in this area covers over 30 elements of HRM and measures of performance. Research into the 'black box' highlights the need to understand *how* and *why* HRM is associated with organisational performance.

◘ There is debate both in theory and in practice about the role of HRM in organisations and about how the HR function might be resourced and organised.

◘ Although the NHS is clearly different from other types of organisation, this does not imply that a new theory of the relationship between HRM and performance is needed, but rather that great care is required when introducing successful approaches or practices that have not already been applied in this context.

◘ There is insufficient evidence to suggest that any single element of HRM is superior to another in terms of its effect on performance.

◘ The HRM–performance link is complex and multi-factorial, and there is little evidence of a direct causal link between HRM and performance.

◘ The nature of the HRM and performance relationship (ie the 'how' and 'why') could be more clearly elaborated.

A quasi-systematic review of empirical literature examined evidence for the link between HRM and performance. Each piece of literature studied met a minimum standard of scientific quality and was published after 1994. Some 97 papers were reviewed in detail, which covered all sectors of business and were international in scope.

The review concluded that there is no agreement about the optimal 'bundle' of HR practices that should be employed by organisations. More than 30 different elements of HRM were used in the papers, and no single element was found to be superior to another in terms of its impact on performance. More than 30 different performance measures were used in the papers, and no single performance measure was dominant.

The papers did not generally make explicit the theoretical perspective used, and in some studies a range of perspectives were used. The majority of papers (up to 80 per cent) used methods which enabled them to show that HRM is *associated with* performance, but could not provide evidence that HRM *causes changes in* performance. The papers primarily relied on questionnaire surveys that used the responses of a single person in the organisation, usually in management.

One characteristic of the NHS is that a large proportion of its staff is professionally qualified. A variety of policies form its strategy – recent focus has been on a patient-centred and patient-led service. Performance management has been formally introduced in the NHS, in parallel with developments in other sectors. The main debate has, however, tended to be about what should be measured, and how, rather than over whether performance should be measured at all.

In terms of HRM, the *HR in the NHS Plan* formed the basis for the development of a variety of HRM policies. Many HR systems and practices stem from national policy, such as the introduction of the national pay spine (*Agenda for Change*), and policy initiatives may be perceived by local NHS employees as a 'one-size-fits-all' approach. Particular local concern was expressed about the

effectiveness of recruitment and retention, pay and rewards, teamworking and communication.

The implications of this research for the NHS in general are that its size can be both a help (in spreading good practice) and a hindrance (in the time taken to implement policies). The transfer of elements of HRM from other sectors demands caution, especially in the light of the changing market economy of the NHS, and the evidence available to support it in the NHS context. The evidence suggests that no single element of HRM will have a dramatic effect on performance. It may therefore be advisable to pursue the benefits of a diversity of approaches.

Research into HRM and performance should take into account the complexities and interplay between elements of HRM, the organisational context, and the limitations of any method used.

A full explanation of terms used in the Report is included in the Glossary (see Appendix 2 on page 89).

1 | Introduction: HRM, the NHS, and performance

Key messages

◨ There has been an increasing interest in the connection between the way people are managed and organisational performance in all sectors, especially in health care, although there is little information currently available for HRM professionals and line managers about how to maximize performance through effective people management.

◨ People management practices are becoming increasingly important within the NHS as the strategy of "Putting patients first, transforming the whole service that people receive and engaging all our staff" (Department of Health, 2005a) impacts at all levels.

◨ The term HRM is used broadly to refer to the management of people within the organization.

◨ The NHS is the largest employer in Europe, and is characterized by a large proportion (about half) of its staff being professionally qualified. In addition, health care is also being delivered by people not employed directly by the NHS – either in partnership or as sub-contractors.

◨ The NHS has a relatively complex structure, and as a public sector organisation it is subject to "constraints, political influence, authority limits, scrutiny and ubiquitous ownership" (Backoff and Nutt, 1992)

◨ There is no consistent or minimum level of local HRM resource within NHS organisations.

This report provides results from the first phase of a research study designed to explore how HRM can contribute to improved performance within the NHS. It is being carried out by a multidisciplinary team who have been at the forefront of both HRM and health policy research, and who have an extensive understanding of leading-edge HR practices in other sectors.

The whole project seeks to:

◨ provide a detailed synthesis of existing knowledge linking HRM to organisational performance – *the focus of this report*

◨ assess the impact of HR practices on performance for different types of services within specific NHS organisations

◘ generate guidance for making HRM decisions that maximise organisational performance. Although there is some information about this in this Report (see p.79), it represents initial observations and will be developed and informed by the second phase of the research.

Human resource management in the NHS

The delivery of health care relies fundamentally upon the human capacity and capabilities of health care organisations to train, develop, deploy, manage and engage their workforce effectively. The centrality of human resource management to health services and health care delivery to patients has been increasingly recognised in the UK in recent years by government, policy-makers, managers, professional organisations and clinical professionals. This has been brought into sharp focus through recent and current health care reforms aimed at modernising the NHS.

Such reforms have included improving access, providing greater choice, promoting innovative and creative new models of service provision, and developing patient-led services. Human resource issues play a central role in each of these initiatives.

The *HR in the NHS Plan* (Department of Health, 2002) was perhaps the most comprehensive and ambitious attempt to create a coherent and comprehensive agenda for action to improve HRM in the NHS. It set out a range of reforms centred on two key aims:

◘ improving the working lives and careers of people working in the NHS, and

◘ improving the efficiency and effectiveness within which health care organisations used the human potential of their workforce.

The aim of the *HR in the NHS Plan* was to achieve *more people, working differently*.

To meet its objectives, the *HR in the NHS Plan* was built on four 'pillars':

◘ making the NHS a model employer

◘ ensuring that the NHS provides a model career through offering a Skills Escalator

◘ improving staff morale

◘ building people management skills.

There has been a host of interrelated reforms and initiatives at a national level to support these objectives since that time, including:

◘ the *New Ways of Working* programme, including the Changing Workforce Programme (to support *working differently*)

◘ the *Improving Working Lives* programme (supporting the development of *the NHS as a model employer*)

◘ four 'modernisations' of aspects of HR to support the development of the *Skills Escalator*:

 − *modernising pay*: new general practitioner and consultant contracts and national pay reforms for other staff through *Agenda for Change*

 − *modernising learning and personal development*: the establishment of the NHS Institute for Innovation and Improvement and the setting up of a number of professional training initiatives

– *modernising regulation*: a focus on all professional groups through a variety of initiatives

– *modernising workforce planning* through the integration of Strategic Health Authorities (SHAs) and Workforce Development Confederations in each area of the country

◘ the introduction of an annual staff survey (to support improving *staff morale*) as well as a variety of initiatives aimed at improving communication

◘ the creation of support networks for HR professionals and the national development of the Electronic Staff Record (to support the *building of people management skills*).

A new workforce strategy was scheduled for the autumn of 2005, and the major themes (around which the detailed strategy will be developed) are already available (Department of Health, 2005b). This document includes the ten high-impact changes for HR listed in Table 1.

Progress is critically dependent on the ability of NHS organisations to take up the opportunities and implement the policies that these reforms entail. As the focus of NHS modernisation increasingly shifts from a national to a local level, people management practices and interventions at the organisational and sub-organisational level gain increasing importance in the reform process.

Seen in a wider context, understanding what works (and *why, how* and *when* it works) in HRM is essential not just for implementing the current reform agenda but for improving health service performance, providing better services for patients, creating better workplaces for staff and bringing about real and lasting improvements in the NHS.

Details of the way in which HR support within the NHS is structured are given on page 7.

HRM and performance

Over the last decade there has been an explosion of interest in the connection between the way people are managed and organisational performance. Empirical studies have found

Table 1 | Ten high-impact changes for HR

Improving organisational efficiency	Improving quality and the patient experience
Effective recruiting, good induction and supportive management to reduce turnover rates	Job and service re-design
Supporting and leading effective change management to save money and prevent service disruption	Appraisal policy development and implementation
Developing shared service models and sharing resources	Staff involvement, partnership working and good employee relations
Managing temporary staffing costs	Championing good people management practices
Promoting staff health and managing sickness absence to boost capacity significantly and improve morale	Effective training and development

> 'Many studies have confirmed an association between HRM and performance ... '

significant relationships between human resource management policies and practices, and various performance outcomes, such as:

- financial turnover (Huselid, 1995; Arthur, 1994)

- productivity (MacDuffie, 1995; Hoque, 1999)

- profits (Delery and Doty, 1996; Huselid, 1995)

- patient mortality (West *et al*, 2002)

- healthcare effectiveness (Borrill *et al*, 2000).

Within the US health sector, research has shown that hospitals able to attract and retain good nursing care (Magnet Hospitals) demonstrate lower mortality rates (Aiken *et al*, 1994).

Many studies have confirmed an association between HRM and performance (with exceptions, eg Wood and deMenezes, 1998). However, the majority of studies that have explored the HRM–performance link (including those in the health sector) do not claim to demonstrate a causal association (Guest *et al*, 2003; West *et al*, 2002). How and in what circumstances HRM is linked to better outcomes has yet to be elaborated.

There is little information for HR professionals who develop HR policies and line managers who implement HR policies about how to maximise performance within the NHS. Research in the field of organisational psychology indicates that the link between HRM and performance is mediated by employee attitudes and behaviours. That is, HR practices trigger attitudes and responses in individuals and encourage them to behave in ways that are consistent with the organisation's overall performance aims (West et al, 2002; Guest *et al*, 2003; Purcell *et al*, 2003).

The specific choice of which practices to include depends on the circumstances affecting each organisation, as well as the interplay between HR professionals and line managers. The effect of policies on individual employees thus becomes an important focus for attention.

It has been argued that the partnership between HR professionals and line managers in the NHS is a critical factor which helps to explain the impact of HR practices and arguably increases their chances of being implemented successfully (Whittaker and Marchington, 2003).

The NHS and its staff

The NHS is the largest employer in Europe, with 1.3 million employees in over 300 careers, in around 600 organisations. The distribution of NHS staff is shown in Figure 1 (Department of Health, 2004a).

The NHS workforce census 2004 covered all staff employed by the NHS (but excluded those employed by subcontractors). It showed significant growth in the numbers of staff overall, doctors, nurses and allied health professionals. Details are shown in Table 2 (Department of Health, 2004a; data rounded to the nearest thousand).

The structure of the NHS

The NHS has a relatively complex structure. It covers a range of organisational types and employs a relatively large number of professional staff. NHS services are increasingly being provided by a range of staff employed by different organisations as opportunities for patient choice increase (Dash, 2004). Mechanisms such as the private finance initiative (PFI) create subcontracts for the provision of health care (Pollock *et al*, 2002).

Figure 1 | The number of staff in the NHS

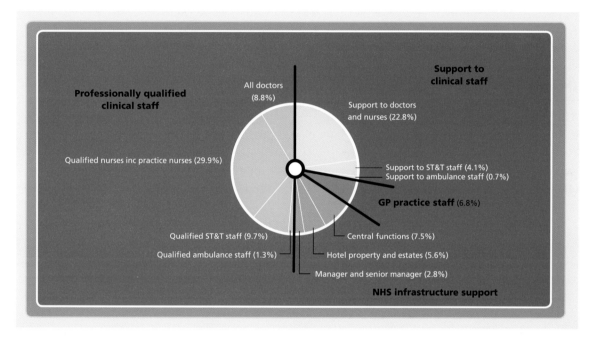

Table 2 | The NHS workforce

1.3 million people were employed in the NHS in September 2004 (on a headcount basis)	Increase of 48,000 since 2003 – an average increase of over 39,000 per year since 1997
Some 661,000 professionally qualified staff	117,000 doctors 398,000 nursing, midwifery and health visiting staff 129,000 scientific, therapeutic and technical staff 17,000 ambulance staff
A further 369,000 staff supporting clinical staff	304,000 supporting doctors and nurses, including nursing assistants, health care assistants , clerical and administrative staff working in clinical areas, porters 55,000 scientific support staff 10,000 ambulance support staff
212,000 staff in infrastructure support	100,000 in central functions, including personnel, finance, IT, library, health education 74,000 in hotel, property and estates 38,000 managers/senior managers
90,000 GP practice staff (excluding nurses, but may include other clinical staff – eg therapists)	

Source: Department of Health 2004a

Organisational structure for the NHS as a whole is shown in Figure 2. It should be noted that this diagram does not indicate employment relationships, which are necessarily more complex.

The role of the Department of Health

As a public sector organisation the NHS has some distinctive characteristics: it is subject to

constraints, political influence, authority limits, scrutiny and ubiquitous ownership.
(Backoff and Nutt, 1992)

The DH performs the 'corporate' function for the NHS by setting overall direction and monitoring progress against objectives. It is also the point at which the NHS interacts directly with the

Government, who vote for resources for the NHS and influence direction.

The DH has recently undergone a process of significant change, and is now focused on (Department of Health, 2004b):

◘ setting the direction of health and social care services in England

◘ setting and monitoring standards for health and social care services

◘ ensuring that NHS and social care organisations have the resources they need

◘ ensuring that patients and the public can make choices about the health and social care services they use.

Figure 2 | The organisational structure of the NHS

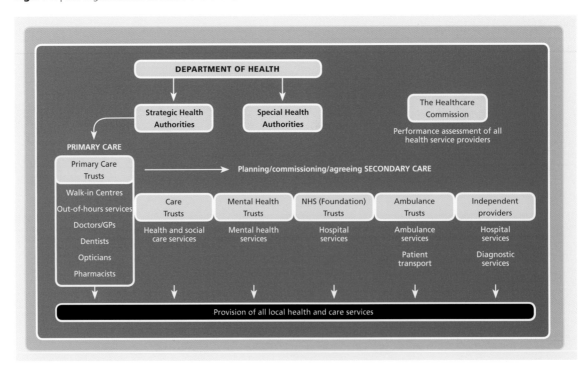

In 2004 the Department completed an 18-month programme of change which reduced the size of the core Department to 2,245 people. It is now structured in three business groups in such a way that the workforce is within the 'Delivery' group (see Table 3).

NHS organisations

A brief description of each type of NHS organisation and its staff is shown in Table 4 on page 8.

HR in the NHS at a national level

The HR Capacity Unit co-ordinates human resources activity in the NHS at a national level. The unit

doesn't simply set benchmarks or impose a single model of HR provision. Instead, it recognises the

need for a 'best fit' approach to organisations that may have a few hundred to a few thousand staff. The HR Capacity Unit is mapping how HR is delivered throughout England, and identifying the different models required.

(Department of Health, 2005c)

NHS Employers was established in 2004 as the employers' organisation for the NHS, and has taken over responsibility for many workforce issues from the DH, as well as supporting and representing the employing organisations (over 600) in the NHS. Its key roles are:

- negotiating on behalf of employers

- representing employers

- supporting employers

- promoting the NHS as an employer.

Table 3 | The structure of the Department of Health

Delivery	Improving the delivery of health and social care services, by monitoring performance and supporting strategic health authorities to improve services and ensure that the NHS has the resources to deliver and develop the workforce strategy for NHS and social care staff. It has six directorates: Access, Finance and investment, Workforce, Programmes and performance, Commercial, and Strategic development
Standards and quality	Setting, maintaining and monitoring standards and quality in the NHS and social care, maintaining and promoting health and well-being, ensuring the safety of patients and service users, and delivering key programmes such as for coronary heart disease and cancer. It has six directorates: Health care quality, Programmes, Research and Development, Care services, Health improvement, and Health protection, international health and scientific development
Strategy and business development	Developing effective DH strategies and managing the Department's business, developing the Department's corporate and management services, nursing, communications, and strategy development. It has four directorates: Corporate management and development, Patient and user experience and involvement and professional leadership, DH communications, and Strategy development

Source: Department of Health 2004b

Table 4 | NHS organisations and employees

Type of organisation	Description	Types of staff
Special Health Authorities	These provide a health service for the whole of England, not just for a local community – for example, the National Blood Authority	Mainly employees of the NHS organisation concerned
Strategic Health Authorities (SHAs)	There are currently 28 SHAs who develop plans for improving health services in their local area, make sure that local health services are of a high quality and are performing well, and make sure that national priorities are integrated into local health service plans. They also take responsibility for workforce development in their area	Staff are employed directly as NHS staff
PRIMARY CARE		
Primary Care Trusts (PCTs)	Primary Care Trusts (PCTs) are organisations responsible for managing health services in a local area. They work with local authorities and other agencies that provide health and social care locally to make sure the community's needs are being met. They do not necessarily employ all the staff who provide these services	PCTs directly employ a small number of staff in managerial positions. The people who provide community nursing services are also directly employed by the PCT. Primary health care services are otherwise delivered by a wide range of independent provider organisations – general practices, community pharmacies, dentists and opticians – who provide services for the NHS under contract and employ their own staff
SECONDARY CARE *Secondary care is provided to treat conditions that cannot normally be dealt with by primary care specialists.*		
Care Trusts	Care Trusts may offer social care, mental health services or primary care services and are set up when the NHS and Local Authorities agree to work closely together	Employment arrangements depend on the individual organisations – it seems that some may second staff from other partner organisations
Mental Health Trusts	Specialist care is normally provided by Mental Health Trusts, often in partnership with other organisations including social services departments and the voluntary sector	Staff are employed by the NHS and social care organisations. Service provision may also depend on other organisations
NHS Trusts	Hospitals are managed by NHS Trusts (also known as Acute Trusts)	Trusts employ most of the NHS workforce. Where Trusts have some form of PFI (49 at present (Department of Health, 2005d), it is possible that a proportion of support staff within the organisation are not directly employed by the NHS
Foundation Trusts	Foundation Trusts are a new type of NHS hospital run by local managers, staff and members of the public which are tailored to the needs of the local population. Foundation Trusts have been given much more financial and operational freedom than other NHS Trusts although they remain within the NHS and its performance inspection system	These employ staff directly
Ambulance Trusts	There are 33 ambulance services covering England, which provide emergency access to health care. In many areas it is the Ambulance Trust which provides transport for patients to get to hospital	Staff are employed by the NHS

Source: Department of Health 2004a

The key areas of work for NHS Employers are:

◘ pay negotiations for NHS staff

◘ employment practice (suspensions, disciplinary framework, health and safety, European issues)

◘ employment policy issues (diversity, healthy workplaces, recruitment and retention initiatives)

◘ Service engagement (including administering networks and the HR in the NHS Conference)

◘ primary medical care contracting.

The DH retains responsibility for developing policy and standards for the health and social care workforce, and has set the broad framework within which NHS Employers operates although it is employers themselves, through the governance structure, who drive the agenda of NHS Employers.

The DH areas of work include:

◘ developing workforce strategy

◘ organising the national HR Capacity Board, including HR directors who provide feedback on key issues

◘ the Social Partnership Forum which engages trade unions on issues other than pay

◘ the HR graduate scheme and HR Leadership schemes to develop capacity for the future

◘ support programmes including an online HR induction programme and an audit tool for assessing whether organisations have the right level of HR capacity

◘ a set of core competencies for HR staff

◘ a research base and a series of master classes with leading academics to develop capability and progressive thinking, as well as close liaison with the CIPD.

A performance measurement system for HR is being rolled out through the development of a HR 'Balanced Scorecard', currently being piloted in seven SHAs. It links outcomes for organisations to better management of people.

A survey of NHS HR staff commissioned in 2003 by the DH suggested that:

◘ the profession was around 10,000 strong

◘ 80 per cent of senior HR staff and 25 per cent of all HR staff had professional qualifications

◘ HR staff are responsible for between 110 members of staff and189 members of staff

◘ most organisations have their own HR function; they are organised differently at local level including some stand-alone functions, and

◘ some are involved in shared service arrangements either as providers or recipients of services.

Local structures and the HR function

There is no standard recommendation for how NHS organisations should be structured – either in primary or secondary care – apart from the requirement to have a Board with an independent Chair, Chief executive, Finance director, Nursing director and Medical director. There are a few statutory subcommittees required of the Board,

> 'It is not possible to compare the functions carried out within hospitals directly with those in a for-profit functionally organised business.'

but apart from that, hospitals are free to design their structures as they deem appropriate.

There appears to be no common structure across NHS Trusts. It is certainly not possible to compare the functions carried out within hospitals directly with those in a for-profit functionally organised business. Most Trusts have an HR function, although they do not all have a director of HR at board level.

Within HR departments there is almost always (certainly at hospital level) someone leading on 'medical staffing' – ie the HR management issues concerned with doctors, as opposed to other types of staff. Although there are some issues that relate specifically to the employment of doctors which might require some specialist support, this type of subdivision of the HR function is not parallelled in other types of non-NHS organisation.

At the primary care level there is even less commonality of structure. Although each PCT has a Board, not all have a director of HR. (Although they do have a representative of HR at Board level, this is not always an HR professional.) Some PCTs have HR services provided through a shared services arrangement, or use shared services for some of the transactional aspects of HR.

Most HR departments place some emphasis on all the main categories of HR activity:

◘ transactional (eg payroll, recruitment advertising)

◘ interventional (eg discipline and grievance)

◘ transformational and strategic work such as service re-design.

Figure 3 | The structure of this report

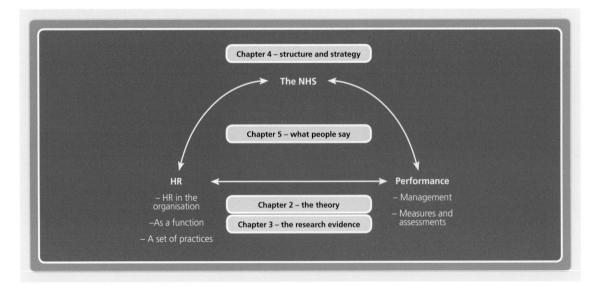

There is currently more emphasis on transformational and strategic work, especially as the policy focus moves towards a patient-led NHS. It has been suggested that there is too much emphasis on transactional and interventional activity.

What this Report contains

This Report considers evidence about the relationship between the NHS, HRM and performance, and the Report is structured as shown in Figure 3. Please note that it does not represent a conceptual framework for the research as a whole – but simply illustrates the structure of this Report.

Table 5 shows where information can be found about the different aspects of the material in this Report.

This Report is the summary of the first phase of a research project and as such it does not make practical suggestions for changes that can result from the data presented here. Instead, it draws out a number of implications for further consideration. It identifies a number of key points which have informed the design of the second phase of the project – which will involve fieldwork in six case-study sites in England drawn from a range of acute, primary care and mental health NHS organisations.

Some key definitions

There is considerable variation in both academic writing and in practice about the meanings of various terms that are used throughout this report. For clarity, these are detailed in Table 6 on page 12.

Table 5 | The contents of this Report

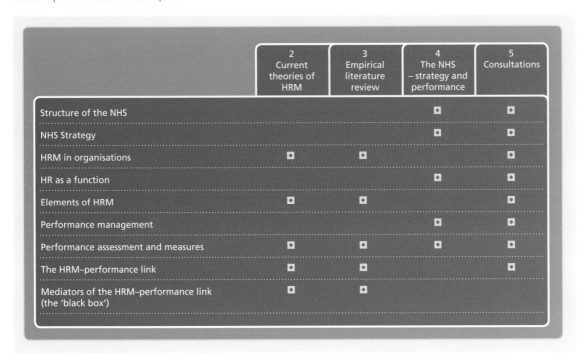

	2 Current theories of HRM	3 Empirical literature review	4 The NHS – strategy and performance	5 Consultations
Structure of the NHS			◘	◘
NHS Strategy			◘	◘
HRM in organisations	◘	◘		◘
HR as a function			◘	◘
Elements of HRM	◘	◘		◘
Performance management			◘	◘
Performance assessment and measures	◘	◘	◘	◘
The HRM–performance link	◘	◘		◘
Mediators of the HRM–performance link (the 'black box')	◘	◘		

The consultations undertaken as part of the study (see Chapter 5) offered insights about how these terms are interpreted in practice, particularly from participants with an HR background, working in the NHS. 'HR' or 'HRM' was categorised as a function within the organisation, whereas 'people management' operated as a more generic term involving line managers.

This view concurs with academic uses of these terms.

Structural arrangements for HRM or personnel management were thought to impact on approaches to people management throughout the organisation. There was also a view that the terms used were irrelevant:

the label doesn't really matter … It is more an issue of how managing people impacts and the effect that it has.

It was also suggested that people there

don't care what it is called as long as it does what it says on the tin.

From personnel to HRM

Participants described a move away from ideas of personnel management towards HRM, describing HRM as having a strategic function in fulfilling organisational goals. The degree of acceptance of HRM as something strategic varied by organisation, and seemed to reflect structural arrangements at Board level.

Table 6 | Key definitions

Human Resources (HR)	Refers to the HR function/department within the organisation. Although 'human resources' are employees, personnel, or the workforce of an organisation, the term is used to refer to an organisational function. Sometimes the term 'HR' is used interchangeably with 'HRM' by staff within organisations (see following paragraph)
Human Resource Management (HRM)	Refers, in general, to the management of people within the organisation, not to a specific function. This includes consideration of the management of people at a strategic level within the organisation
HR practices	A set of practices used to manage the workforce of an organisation – ie recruitment, selection, training, involvement, usually promoted by the HR function. The term 'elements of HRM' is also used to refer to these practices
People management	Refers to all aspects of how people are managed by line managers. It involves broader activities than those carried out by the HR function
Employees	Refers to individuals working within, and employed under an employment contract by, the organisation. Although the legal definition of such people is as 'worker', it is not normally associated with managerial work
High-performance paradigm	Describes the overall concept of the relationship between HRM and organisational performance
The 'black box'	Describes the factors that mediate the link between HRM and performance

There have been big changes in the NHS over the past 30 years. HR now has an increase in voting rights as a member of the Board. There is an emphasis on having HR with the CEO and finance and other directors. IT and planning rights have been transferred to HR.

(HR director)

There was a suggestion that 'personnel management' was more understandable as a description of the work.

'HR' is an Americanism. I prefer 'personnel management'. Most people don't understand the difference. Most just see HR as a modern way to do personnel management.

(HR manager)

One account suggested an increased influence from HR as a function:

There is a realisation that clinical managers need support from specialists. HR practitioners moved from being policemen to transactional staff and providing a supporting role. The result is that we are beginning to impress clinicians that HR understands the business... When we have explained that we could work in HR elsewhere and earn more money, and that we are also dedicated to patient care, then we have become seen as just as committed as clinicians. Most HR practitioners in the NHS believe they make a contribution to patient care. They are interested in how what they do impacts on the frontline. They had to crow-bar themselves in, but to learn to talk the talk, speak the right language.

(HR manager)

People management

People management was described as 'everyone's concern' in an organisation because all employees – particularly line-managers – retain responsibility for people management. It was suggested that by using the term 'people management', elements of HRM could be better integrated within the organisation and that relationships between HR and clinical staff might be affected positively.

The NHS is not aware of what HRM is but it is aware of people management. To the NHS HR equals a narrow set of roles. This is different, depending on what Trust you are in. The people side of the equation is seen as an 'add-on'. PCTs seem different because they have a different outlook from front line-staff. HR are seen as performance coaches and are a member of the senior team and Board.

(HR director in a PCT)

2 | Current theories of HRM

Key messages

◘ There are three main perspectives on the high-performance paradigm (the overall concept of the relationship between HR practices and organisational performance):

- 'best practice' (otherwise known as high commitment)

- 'best fit' (alternatively known as a 'contingency' model), which argues that to experience competitive advantage, 'progressive' HR practices must be aligned with business strategy

- the 'resource based view', which focuses on the internal resources at the disposal of the employer as opposed to treating factors external to the organisation as the main driver of HRM, and has a key focus on adding value and competitive position.

◘ The content of current research in this area is concerned both with the elements of HRM studied and with measures of performance.

◘ Approaches to research into the 'black box' of employee attitudes and behaviour vary but can be broadly classified as being focused on employee motivation and discretionary effort, commitment to the organisation, the psychological contract, the importance of culture and managerial influence, highlighting the need to understand how and why HRM is associated with organisational performance.

While the majority of analyses of these kinds of HRM models tend to focus on the private sector (and to be concerned with the means of maximising productivity through managing employees in a particular way), they are still particularly relevant to HRM in the NHS. This chapter is divided into three sections focusing on the literature, the content and design of current research in this area, and approaches to research into the 'black box'.

An overview of HRM and performance literature

The idea that HRM has an impact on performance – either at an individual or an organisational level – has long attracted the interest of both academics and practitioners. Since being seen in its early days as little more than a welfare function, designed to act as an intermediary between managerial and non-managerial staff, HRM is now perceived as a key factor for improved organisational performance.

> 'A number of competing theoretical perspectives ... go to the heart of how HRM and performance are defined and measured ...'

When examining the HRM–performance link, a number of competing theoretical perspectives have to be assessed because they go to the heart of how HRM and performance are defined and measured, how the links operate between them, and how any obstacles preventing the conversion of HRM into practice might be overcome.

While it is accepted that the relationship is neither simple nor direct, its potential impact on employee satisfaction and commitment is a forerunner for higher levels of quality and productivity. In the case of the NHS this is translated into improved levels of patient care at similar or reduced cost.

High-commitment HRM and best practices

'Best practice' HRM offers a universalist view in which the adoption of a certain set of HR practices will benefit organisations. These prescriptions follow the principle (Purcell, 1999; p.26)

that all firms can and should adopt a set of human resource management practices for the combined benefit of the firm and its employees.

This has become the dominant theme in many recent studies, as researchers, policy-makers and practitioners have sought to identify a set of HR practices that have a universal effect on performance (Arthur, 1994; Huselid, 1995; Youndt *et al*, 1996; Wood and deMenezes, 1998; Guest *et al*, 2000; Guest *et al*, 2003; West *et al*, 2002).

A number of these have shown strong support for the idea that specific sets, or 'bundles', of HR practices do have a beneficial effect on a range of employee and organisational outcomes – such as improved levels of commitment, quality or productivity, and even profits (see, for example,

Huselid, 1995; Guest *et al*, 2000; Guest *et al*, 2003; Patterson *et al*, 1997).

HR bundles

Many studies have identified the role that 'bundles' of HR practices – a set of interlocking and mutually reinforcing practices – can play in improving the motivation, satisfaction and commitment of employees, and thus performance. Different views exist about whether or not it is the greater the number of HR practices that matters or if all of the practices must be in place before HRM is effective.

Appealing though this line of inquiry might be to employers keen to achieve improved performance, it also has several shortcomings (Marchington and Wilkinson, 2005). For example:

- It is unclear which HR practices constitute the appropriate 'bundle' of best practice techniques.

- The fact that there is no universally agreed theory about HRM makes comparison difficult. Equally, the fact that the studies have been conducted in different countries and in different industries hinders comparison.

- Many studies rely on survey data that is not always sensitive enough to variations in organisational practice or circumstances, and make little allowance for gradations in how HR practices are implemented by line managers (Purcell *et al*, 2003).

'Best fit … argues that to experience competitive advantage, 'progressive' HR practices
need to be aligned with business strategy …'

◘ Although there have been problems in
identifying the composition of an effective
HR bundle, there have also been variations
in the proxies that are used for assessing
performance, and there has been a tendency
to focus on universal indicators such as profits,
productivity or quality.

◘ Moreover, although there may be statistically
significant associations between high-
commitment HRM and performance, it is rarely
acknowledged that such practices tend to be
more costly to implement and therefore have
to deliver higher levels of performance in order
to pay for themselves (Cappelli and Neumark,
2001).

So while the implementation of a high-
commitment HRM might make sense for a whole
variety of reasons, it should not be assumed
that it will impact positively on performance
in all organisations.

If 'best practice' results in superior organisational
performance, why is it that some companies that
do not employ such 'bundles' of HR practices still
perform well (Wood and deMenezes, 1998)? And
more importantly, why do so few firms embrace
best practice?

> Pfeffer, 1998 suggests a simple '$\frac{1}{8}$ rule',
> according to which half the people will not act
> on the connection between high-performance
> work systems (HPWS)/HRM and profitability,
> half of those who do act will try a single
> (one-shot) solution rather than a systematic
> approach, and only a half of the firms that
> do make systematic changes will persist long
> enough to see the difference ($\frac{1}{2} \times \frac{1}{2} \times \frac{1}{2} = \frac{1}{8}$).

Although this figure is remarkably close to the
proportion of workplaces who embraced HPWS
(14 per cent, Cully et al, 1999; p.295), important
factors limiting the widespread adoption of 'best
practice' would appear to be:

◘ managerial competence

◘ different opinions about the most appropriate
approach towards employees (eg coercion or
co-operation)

◘ competition in the product market

◘ pressures from financial markets that favour
short-term as opposed to long-term HRM
strategies (eg cost-cutting rather than
investment in training and development)

◘ conflicts of interest between management and
labour (Blyton and Turnbull, 2004; p.114–28).

It will be interesting to see whether there have
been any changes in the proportion of workplaces
embracing HPWS, especially in the light of the
introduction of new or reformed legislation since
1997 in a number of areas that could be classified
under a high-performance paradigm – for
example, changes in working hours, rates of pay,
union recognition, work and family life, workplace
conflict, equal opportunities and information and
communication. Initial findings suggest that there
might be a slight increase.

This leads Purcell (1999; p.36) to conclude that the
idea of universalism leads us into a utopian cul-de-
sac. Thus indicating a 'best fit' approach to HRM
may be more successful.

From an NHS perspective, best practice approaches
may be provided via national policies, which
stipulate the direction of HRM locally.

Adopting a universal model of HRM practices is complicated within the NHS, partly due to the wide range of organisations and employment relationships, and the divergent nature of the various staff groups represented.

Contingency and best fit models

An alternative to the best practice approach suggests that HRM should adapt to the specific organisational context. Best fit – otherwise known as a contingency approach – argues that to experience competitive advantage, 'progressive' HR practices need to be aligned with business strategy (Miles and Snow, 1984; Barney, 1991; Barney, 1995; Huselid, 1995; Delery et al, 1997).

Analysis of indicative factors is used to determine which practices are required in conjunction with core HR practices. Drawing on contingency theory, it is argued that HRM depends upon factors such as organisational structure, size and complexity, as well as external factors such as technology, product and labour market circumstances, and economic, political and legal climate (see Figure

4). In addition, it depends on the goals the organisation is setting out to achieve.

What this means in practice is that 'ideal' HR practices will vary greatly in different situations.

A number of models have been developed in order to identify how HRM might vary according to organisational circumstances (Marchington and Wilkinson, 2005; Schuler and Jackson, 1987; Delery and Doty, 1996; Sisson and Storey, 2000). It has been argued that whereas this version of HRM might be relevant to organisations that compete on the basis of quality, it is unrealistic to expect those organisations that need to reduce costs to implement such policies. Distinctions are also made between HRM in organisations whose growth has been through acquisition and divergence and those who have retained a strong commitment to one particular market and sector.

In other words, HRM does and should vary dramatically between organisations depending on their strategies and circumstances.

Figure 4 | Factors that affect management choices in HR strategy

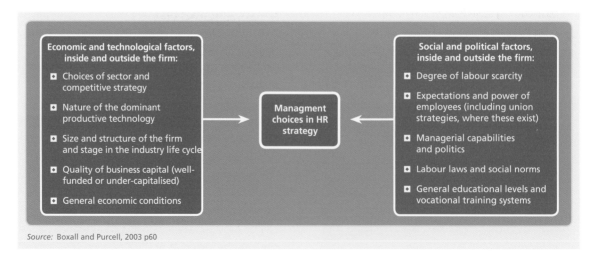

Source: Boxall and Purcell, 2003 p60

The best fit approach is intuitively attractive, especially to UK organisations that place an emphasis on flexibility. However, there are also difficulties in this approach that have been identified:

◘ The approach implies that suitable HRM can be easily determined from an analysis of organisational objectives and contextual circumstances.

◘ 'Best fit' tends to overlook employee interests (Boxall and Purcell, 2003) and fails to identify the importance of aligning employee interests with appropriate HR practices (Boxall, 1996; Coff, 1997; Lees, 1997).

◘ In addition to ignoring the societal context in which employers operate, it assumes that organisations are like machines and that employees (and managers, for that matter) do not have any influence on how HRM is adopted.

◘ It also ignores the fact that different 'external' circumstances send signals that can be interpreted by employers in different ways, and that one may be calling for a tough cost-cutting style (say, when competition is tight) whereas another might suggest a high-commitment style (say, in times of skills shortages).

◘ Moreover, the approach assumes that employers are able to implement similar (or different) styles depending on contingencies without there being any interaction between parts of the organisation and without any consequences for HRM, reputation or profitability. For example, it may be feasible to acknowledge economic factors facing an organisation, but beyond the organisation's power to affect them. While this approach is in some ways more locally specific than best practice, it does not necessarily follow that the HR function will become more effective in what it sets out to achieve.

◘ If managers find it difficult to follow a 'one-size-fits-all' or 'best practice' formula, to what extent will they be able to identify – let alone model – all the contingent variables they face? How might they evaluate all the interconnections, and implement the 'best fit' solution? Purcell (1999; p.31) suggests that this idea is nothing more than a chimera. The reality is more likely to be a situation in which organisations 'react to particular circumstances as best they can' (Edwards, 1986; p.41), with HR practices 'following' the market rather than 'fitting' the business strategy.

◘ Finally, unlike studies of best practice, there has been relatively limited empirical work on best fit, and existing findings are contradictory.

This approach may, however, prove useful in identifying the institutional factors that both shape and constrain HR practices in the NHS.

Resource-based views

Resource-based views (RBVs) offer a similar perspective to best fit approaches in that they acknowledge that the most effective models of HRM might vary between organisations. The difference lies between focusing on the internal resources at the disposal of the employer as opposed to treating factors external to the organisation as the main driver of HRM.

Drawing on strategic management theory (Penrose, 1959; Barney, 1995), RBV has been

'**Resource-based approaches blend organisational, economic and strategic management ...**'

applied in the area of HRM and suggests that the potential for sustained competitive advantage or long-run superior performance rests upon four specific attributes (Boxall and Purcell, 2003). These are applied to HRM in the following way:

◘ *value* – that HRM must be capable of adding value to the organisation in some way that other resources do not (eg through employee involvement or discretionary behaviour)

◘ *rarity* – that human resources of the necessary calibre are in short supply and have to be retained (eg through careful selection and retention policies)

◘ *imperfect imitability* – that HR practices and processes, as well as staff, are not capable of being copied by other organisations (eg teamworking/high-quality staff)

◘ *irreplaceability* – that they are not substitutable

by other factors which make them obsolete (eg through replacement by machines or subcontractors).

Resource-based approaches blend organisational, economic and strategic management, advocating that for organisations to be successful they must gain and sustain competitive advantage (Porter, 1985). Sustained competitive advantage is distinguished from competitive advantage (Barney, 1995). Achieving sustained competitive advantage is effected by acquiring resources that are non-substitutable, inimitable, rare and valuable (Wright *et al*, 1994). Such achievements become a focus for HRM in the development of people in the organisation (Barney, 1995; Pfeffer, 1994; Wright *et al*, 1994; Truss, 2001).

There are three main types of resources that may be used:

◘ physical resources (ie technology and equipment)

Figure 5 | Employment modes and relationships

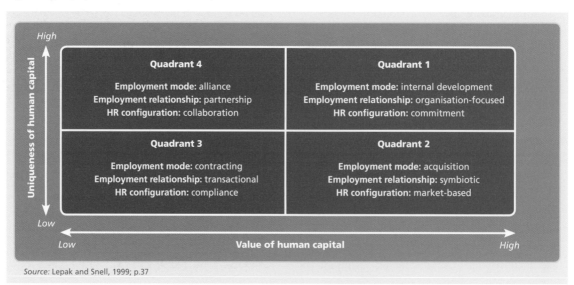

Source: Lepak and Snell, 1999; p.37

◪ human resources (experience and knowledge of people in the organisation)

◪ organisational resources (structure, systems planning, monitoring and controlling).

Like best fit approaches the RBV is difficult for employers to enact. Moreover, because it refers to long-term developments in organisations, it is not something that can be picked up easily by other employers and used as a benchmark for change.

The NHS may experience political difficulties – ie separating out one group of staff for special treatment in an organisation where HRM (say, in terms of pay levels, training opportunities or career advancement) is highly visible to other employees and where work in cross-functional teams is critically important for the achievement of organisational goals.

This approach is made more difficult when performance is dependent upon the close co-operation of staff from a number of different agencies and employers (Marchington *et al*, 2004).

Variations in employee skills and knowledge have been categorised by Lepak and Snell (1999) – see Figure 5 – who distinguish between the level of human capital required to undertake a job and the 'uniqueness' of the skill needed. They emphasise the subsequent 'managerial' variations that are likely to develop. The NHS has employees in each of the quadrants (Purcell *et al*, 2003; p.707).

Table 7 | A summary of 'Best Practice' in HRM Literature

(Arthur, 1994)	(Pfeffer, 1994)	(Delaney et al., 1989, Huselid, 1995)	(MacDuffie, 1995)	(Delery and Doty, 1996)
Broadly defined jobs	Employment security	Labour/management participation	Training of experienced employees	Internal career promotion
Stock ownership	Symbolic egalitarianism	Performance appraisal	Problem-solving groups	Job descriptions
Employee participation	Selective recruiting	Incentive compensation	Employee suggestions	Formal training
Formal dispute resolution	High wages	Job design	Job rotation	Appraisals
Information-sharing	Incentive pay	Grievance procedures	Decentralisation	Profit-sharing
Highly skilled employees	Employee ownership	Information-sharing	Recruitment and hiring	Employment security
Self-managed teams	Information sharing	Attitude assessment	Contingent compensation	Participation
Extensive training	Participation	Recruiting intensity	Status differentiation	
Extensive benefits	Empowerment	Training hours	Training of new employees	
High wages	Promotion from within	Promotion criteria (seniority v merit)	Work teams	
Salaried employees	Job redesign/teams	Personnel selection		
	Cross-training and skills development			
	Cross-utilisation			
	Wage compression			

Source: Youndt et al, 1996, p840

It should be noted that, in common with other models, there is a tendency to assume that individual organisations have considerable autonomy to choose approaches to HRM that suit them best without any consideration of wider implications for the sector in which they operate or for society at large. This is not always the case, especially in public sector organisations.

It is difficult to see how this approach could be applied to the NHS. The competitive environment is different from the private sector. For example, it would not be possible for many NHS organisations to focus only on what they are 'good' at, because that could entail discontinuing services which are required by the local community. However, specialised NHS organisations which have a particular strength may be able to focus more on these, developing their own 'unique' characteristics while other aspects of a local health economy could ensure that no essential service became unavailable. Such an approach may be possible, for example, for Foundation Hospitals.

Current research – content and design

Elements of HRM

The implementation of a set of practices or elements of HRM forms the core of the best practice approach. Types of HR practices that have been identified as contributing to this performance effect have varied and are shown in Table 7. Some studies focus on the role of training and development, others on employee involvement and job design or some form of variable pay. Remaining studies have suggested that careful selection and employment security are what really matters.

HR practices typically identified in the 'best practice' literature include:

◘ recruitment policies

◘ employee involvement

◘ training

◘ performance-related pay

◘ performance appraisals

◘ job security

(Huselid, 1995; MacDuffie, 1995; Wood and Albanese, 1995; Patterson *et al*, 1997; Appelbaum *et al*, 2000).

These practices

comprise the work system that enables employees to use their skills and motivation to maximum benefit.
Delery *et al,* 1997; p5

For example, West *et al* (2002) suggested the influence that training, teamworking and appraisal played in reducing mortality following surgery.

Measures of performance

Thus far this Report has focused on HR practices (the *inputs* to the 'black box'). Equally, there has been considerable debate on precisely how to measure performance (the *outputs* from the 'black box'). Early research focused solely on improvements to financial performance (Devanna *et al*, 1984; Tichy *et al*, 1982). However, the purpose of HRM is not just to improve financial performance (Legge, 1995). Advocates of HRM/ HPWS suggest that these policies also provide a number of positive outcomes for *employees* (eg a rewarding place to work, a sense of security, involvement and identity with the organisation, opportunities for personal development, and the like).

Measures of performance include:

- employee motivation

- commitment

- decreases in turnover

- training levels

- absenteeism rates

- the output of goods and services – more specifically the units produced, the number of customers served, the number of errors and customer complaints

- time, incorporating employee lateness, the occurrence of absenteeism, and examination of any failures to meet deadlines

- financial indicators, assessment of which can generate an array of possible indicators.

This has led to the use of a 'balanced scorecard' approach (Guest, 1997; Ulrich, 1997; Benkhoff, 1997; Purcell, 1999), reflecting the needs and objectives of all major stakeholders (eg shareholders, managers, customers and

employees). It has been argued that this offers a more appropriate system of measurement than a simple focus on financial indicators (Kaplan and Norton, 1992).

The link between HRM and performance

Little is known, specifically, about how and why HR practices impact on organisational performance. A number of explanations have been proposed, focusing on the individual factors comprising the 'black box':

Discretionary effort

The effort employees are willing to put in has been understood through theories of motivation incorporating elements of high commitment and high involvement and models of discretionary effort.

To establish competitive advantage, effort above and beyond what is required by employees to fulfil the job must be exerted. This is known as *discretionary effort* (Bailey, 1993) which involves

more than simply getting people to work harder … Rather, the objective is to get employees to apply their creativity and imagination as well as to exploit their intimate, and often unconscious, knowledge of the work process.
(Bailey, 1993; pp.5–6)

Discretionary effort might be used to explain how potential labour is converted into performed labour. Discretionary effort comprises three components, namely motivation, skills and opportunities to participate (Appelbaum *et al*, 2000). See Figure 6 below.

Employees need incentives to motivate them to exert discretionary effort. This increased level of motivation will be wasted, however, unless employees possess the necessary skills to make their extra effort meaningful (Appelbaum *et al*, 2000).

Finally, employees need opportunities to participate, thereby providing a forum for their extra motivation and skills. By enabling these three components, levels of commitment, trust and communication are thought to increase. 'Bundles' of HR practices focused on incentives, skills and opportunities to participate, result in employees exerting discretionary effort, which in turn results in improved individual and organisational performance (Delaney and Huselid 1996; Huselid, 1995). Following this approach appears

to present a step forward in theorising about linkages.

(Truss, 2001; p.1127)

Human motivation involves a complex network of human interaction involving trust, support, recognition and respect. Care should be taken because models of motivation within HRM frequently overlook issues outside HRM – ie the costs of implementation of HR practices and organisational emphasis on short-term rather than long-term planning.

Purcell *et al* (2003) examined the impact of people management on organisational performance. Findings from 12 organisations from a range of sectors suggested that performance is a function of ability, motivation and opportunity (AMO). Pass (2004) studied discretionary effort through the triangulation of employee attitude surveys, focus groups and participant observations. Her findings suggested that discretionary effort arose from respect, recognition and relationships amongst workers.

In addition to effort, commitment plays a vital role in linking HRM with performance. Commitment can be affected significantly by the actions of multiple employers, not just by the direct link between employer and employee (Rubery *et al*, 2002). Little is known about whether or not

Figure 6 | Three components of discretionary effort

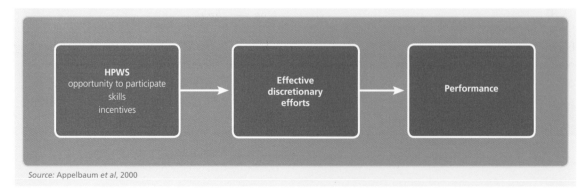

Source: Appelbaum *et al*, 2000

'Employment relationships of those providing patient care is complicated because control and responsibility extends across organisational boundaries'

employees transferred from the public sector continue to hold a public sector ethos that benefits patients directly (Hebson *et al*, 2003).

In the health care sector, a proportion of people are employed by organisations other than the NHS (eg either through private companies in a PFI, social services, or voluntary/charitable organisations). Employment relationships of those providing patient care is complicated because control and responsibility extends across organisational boundaries. NHS organisations have also to gain the commitment of these other organisations.

The psychological contract

The employee–employer relationship is an essential component of HRM. The concept of the psychological contract has been used to explore this relationship. It can account for attitudes and affective responses of individual employees and employers. It has been suggested that a strong psychological contract may result in a healthier, happier, and perhaps more productive workforce (Sparrow and Cooper, 2003).

Nurses who perceived that they were valued by the organisation reported better health than those who felt undervalued.
(Bradley and Cartwright, 2002)

Breach of the psychological contract, on the other hand, occurs, for example, when employees perceive that their organisation has failed to meet one or more of its obligations. Such breaches can have a detrimental effect on the attitudes and responses of employees (Morrison and Robinson, 1997). Organisational failure to meet employee obligations is also associated with emotional exhaustion and job dissatisfaction (Gakovic and Tetrick, 2003).

The psychological contract in the NHS is an example of context-specific HRM where a closer relationship between people at the top of an organisation and staff is crucial to enhanced performance (Caulkin, 2003; Purvis and Cropley, 2003).

Culture

The NHS is a multicultural society. Each profession – medical, nursing, management, and many others – has its own identity, culture and subcultures. Within medicine there are various specialty groupings, such as surgeons, psychiatrists, or general practitioners, with different characteristics and aims. The potential for conflict arising from cultural differences is almost limitless – a problem not, of course, unique to the NHS.
(Drife and Johnson, 1995)

A number of factors mediate HRM and performance. There is an increasing body of work on the link between organisational culture and performance, from HRM (Sparrow and Cooper, 2003) and specific to the NHS (Mannion *et al*, 2005). The culture–performance link is contingent on other factors such as HRM.

Line managers

The importance of line managers for implementing HR practices has been identified as a key feature of the HRM–performance link. Most HR practices are 'brought to life' by line managers, and their willingness to do this depends on their discretion (Purcell *et al*, 2003). However, in the NHS, and the public sector generally, the capacity and capability

> 'There has been a lack of substantial information from the employee perspective.'

of managers to implement new policy forms only part of the challenge facing them during an era of major organisational change (Vere and Beaton, 2003). Thus HRM must take into account the needs of and resources required for those individuals tasked with applying policy to practice.

Research design

Research into the high-performance paradigm has been conducted predominantly in the manufacturing sector (Arthur, 1994; Pfeffer, 1994; MacDuffie, 1995), and has, for the most part, been conducted in the USA and UK.

Research studies have tended to rely on survey data where:

- most information comes from a single management respondent who provides data on both HR practices and various measures of organisational performance

- the HR practices studies are often then 'bundled' together by different authors into different combinations where, perhaps, the statistically significant variables are identified from a regression equation.

There has been a lack of substantial information from the employee perspective. Studies to date have assumed that if employers report HR policies that are part of the high-commitment paradigm, these will automatically result in positive outcomes for employees because they enhance their working lives.

For example, it is usually assumed that employee involvement and teamwork are positive for employees because they provide greater opportunities to receive information, influence management and make decisions with less supervisory intervention. Consultation with employees can offer valuable insights:

Studying employees' attitudes and experiences with workplace practices can help researchers get 'inside the black box' between inputs and outputs in the production process. It can improve our understanding of the ways in which HPWS are related to performance.

(Appelbaum *et al*, 2000; p.110)

Following this line of reasoning it is suggested that employees will want to be involved, and that this will lead to improvements in performance. However, it has been argued that rather than liberating and empowering employees, such practices might intensify their work by:

- forcing them to expend extra effort without any commensurate increase in remuneration

- coercion to contribute to management objectives with which they do not agree

- engaging in competition with other teams to gain recognition from management

(Ramsay *et al*, 2000; Godard, 2004; Bacon and Blyton, 2005).

These actions may therefore not be in the best interests of employees who may take on managerial objectives and so end up losing an independent voice (Harley *et al*, 2005). In much the same way:

- selective hiring may result in the exclusion of employees who do not fit with the dominant norms in an organisation

◘ training may be extensive in quantity but not valuable in adding to employee skills

◘ variable pay might be good for those that gain but lead to increasing tensions between groups of employees who are meant to collaborate on joint projects.

Much, of course, depends on the way that management seeks to implement and embed HRM in the workplace, as well as on the attitudes of the employees themselves to new initiatives. Inconsistencies and contradictions about the application of HRM can give the impression that managers are neither professional nor to be trusted.

Without research on employees' views, it is unclear whether high-performance practices result in either work intensification or job satisfaction. As a result, studies of employee responses are a legitimate study in their own right (Guest, 1999). Without data from employees on their experiences of work we will only learn of the rhetoric of HRM and lose sight of the reality (Legge, 1995; Truss, 2001).

As already indicated, 'middle managers' are central to HRM because of increased devolution of responsibility (Guest, 1987; Legge, 1989). Studies have highlighted the importance of middle managers in effective HRM (Currie and Procter, 2001; p.65), mainly because of their position of influence in the implementation of HR practices (Currie, 1999). However, the devolution of responsibility to middle managers has been far from seamless because of:

◘ ambiguity about how processes work in practice (McGovern *et al*, 1997; Currie and Procter 2001)

◘ a lack of preparation (Marchington and Wilkinson, 2000)

◘ inadequate training of middle management to handle the increased responsibility (Cunningham and Hyman, 1999; p.18)

◘ the attitudinal beliefs of middle managers (Cunningham and Hyman, 1995; Lupton, 2000)

◘ a lack of support from the HR department (Whittaker and Marchington, 2003).

There is little empirical data on devolution, on the impact on middle managers, and especially on employees under the influence of these middle managers. What is evident is that middle managers have a highly influential role in the implementation of HR practices on the ground. Although appraisals, communication, pay, benefits, and health and safety form part of a middle manager's role, they still have considerable influence on the impact of other HR practices. Employee experiences of HR practices will be influenced by their experience of the middle manager, and it is therefore important to consider the relationship between middle management and employees when considering employee opinions of HRM (Hutchinson and Wood, 1995; Hope-Hailey *et al*, 1997; Torrington and Hall, 1998; Whittaker and Marchington, 2003).

3 | Research evidence

Key messages

◻ Over 30 different elements of HRM were researched in this literature review. There was no single dominant element of HRM and there is insufficient evidence to suggest that any one element of HRM may be superior to another in terms of its impact on performance.

◻ Training, pay, involvement and 'bundles' all featured as having the most significant associations with performance, however, pay, involvement and 'bundles' were also found to have the most negative associations with performance. Evidence on the links between pay and performance is very mixed, despite the relatively large number of studies.

◻ Over 30 performance measures were used. There was no single dominant performance measure.

◻ Relatively few studies explored the full link between HRM–black box–performance. Some papers reported that commitment, trust, skill, attitudes and motivation were important.

◻ The studies did not in general make explicit the theoretical perspective used. In some studies more than one perspective was used.

◻ Empirical studies used, primarily, questionnaire surveys with a single management respondent, and made little use of other sources of data.

◻ Research has been primarily carried out and published in the UK or the US with over half covering more than one industry. Single industry studies included manufacturing, telecommunications/IT or finance

◻ The majority of papers (>80%) used cross-sectional samples with correlation or regression analysis, which shows that HRM is associated with performance, but could not provide evidence that HRM caused changes in performance.

The previous chapter demonstrated that the relationship between human resource practices/policies/systems/strategies (referred to here as 'elements of HRM') and performance has been a longstanding concern not only of HR professionals but of organisations generally. Any evidence may affect investment decisions that direct resources towards those HRM practices most likely to impact on improved organisational performance.

This chapter examines the empirical evidence (from research literature) that can help us to understand which elements of HRM lead to high performance

Our examination of the empirical evidence addresses the following questions:

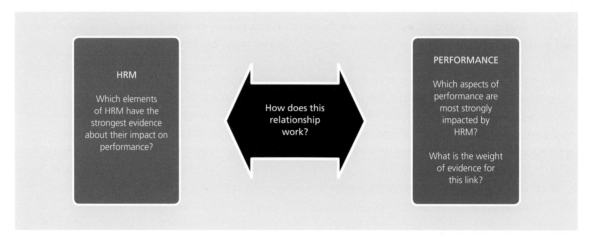

Finding the evidence

Methods for reviewing the literature about a subject as diffuse as the relationship between HRM and performance are relatively underdeveloped (Sheaff *et al*, 2004). There is a vast quantity of literature in this area, which involves a range of research methods (see, for example, Boselie *et al*, 2005). Systematic review guidelines offered a source of good practice for this examination. Systematic reviews have three stages, which were used in this study:

(a) Developing a search strategy and conducting the searches.

This yielded approximately 13,000 papers (of which about 10 per cent were duplicated across databases).

(b) Developing and using a set of inclusion/exclusion criteria for the papers found in the searches (this involves scanning the abstract of each paper found to determine whether it should be examined in detail in the following stage of the process).

This reduced the 13,000 papers to 367 which were potentially relevant.

(c) Developing and using a data extraction template to further refine the selection of papers (this involves reading each paper and classifying its contents using the template).

All 367 were read and this yielded the final 97 papers on which the analysis in this chapter is based.

Details of these stages and full details of the review are available from the authors; these provide a data source for researchers and practitioners seeking to identify the range of performance measures and specific HRM practices/polices/strategies and systems used to explore the HRM–performance links.

The search terms 'human resource [management]' and 'performance' or 'productivity' were used in three databases. In refining the search, organisational performance measures were sought, rather than those specific to HRM, on the basis that this research was designed to explore how HRM might impact on organisational performance in general. Although it is recognised that many measures of HRM effectiveness – eg absence, labour turnover – do have an impact on the overall financial performance of the organisation, the focus here is on the contribution of HRM to the effectiveness of the business.

A breakdown of the final number of papers judged as suitable for inclusion in this review (97) and their source database is shown in Table 8.Throughout this chapter the 97 included papers are referred to as 'the empirical papers'; they are

the ones on which all the subsequent analysis has been conducted.

Components of the papers

In this section various components of the empirical papers are described:

◘ the elements of HRM used

◘ the performance measures used

◘ the sources of the evidence for the various elements of HRM and performance measures used

◘ the context in which the studies have been conducted

◘ the research designs.

It has not been possible to categorise the papers found in terms of the theoretical perspective employed, despite attempts to do so. Most of the papers made no reference at all to the theoretical perspective used, and many seemed to use aspects of more than one perspective so that classification into a single category was not possible.

The elements of HRM used and the source of the evidence

In total, 31 different HRM practice or policy measures were used in the papers. Figure 7 on page 32 shows the 10 most frequently used HRM practices/policies in terms of the percentage of papers using those practices. Although 14.5 per cent of papers used composites of these measures (termed 'bundles' or 'indexes' in the papers), we have included the separate variables used within these composites to illustrate the wide range of measures used.

Table 8 | Papers included in the empirical review

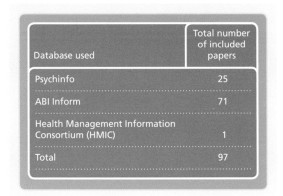

Database used	Total number of included papers
Psychinfo	25
ABI Inform	71
Health Management Information Consortium (HMIC)	1
Total	97

The most commonly used measure was training and development (50.5 per cent of n = 49). This was followed by: pay/compensation, employee involvement, selection and recruitment processes and teamworking. These five practices are mirrored in a well-known list of seven HRM practices (Pfeffer, 1994), although the remaining two (employment security/internal promotion and reduction of status differentials) were ranked much lower in this review, coming in as the fifteenth and eighteenth most commonly used measures respectively.

There is no single element of HRM that was consistently used to examine the HRM–performance link.

Studies gathered evidence from a variety of sources:

◘ The majority of studies (n = 76) use only one subjective data source (ie one individual), usually collected using a questionnaire, to gain information about the elements of HRM. The data for 61 of these studies was obtained from managers, the remainder being focused on a mixture of employees and line managers.

◘ 49 studies used the same (single) source to obtain performance measurement data.

◘ Four studies used more than one method or source to obtain information about the elements of HRM.

◘ Five studies used objective measures, such as databases, to obtain information about the elements of HRM practices.

◘ Thirteen used more than one data source in the organisation to gain differing perspectives on the information.

It should be noted that:

◘ Not all measures are equally easy to quantify.

For example, how much someone gets paid, or how many part-time employees are employed at any one time may be easier to quantify and the judgements of one individual might be acceptable for this type of data collection. However, other measures are not as tangible – eg the extent of employee involvement or teamworking. It is therefore more difficult for individuals to judge

Figure 7 | Elements of HRM used in the empirical papers

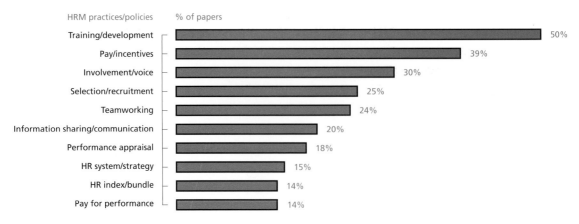

HRM practices/policies	% of papers
Training/development	50%
Pay/incentives	39%
Involvement/voice	30%
Selection/recruitment	25%
Teamworking	24%
Information sharing/communication	20%
Performance appraisal	18%
HR system/strategy	15%
HR index/bundle	14%
Pay for performance	14%

whether and how much that practice is occurring, and there is more likely to be disagreement where more than one individual is asked to make a judgement.

◘ There may be bias in those determining the ratings.

For example, the source questioned (eg the HR manager) may be likely to depict a positive perspective of his/her practices and policies but that does not necessarily represent reality for front line staff. This could be ameliorated by using two or more sources and measuring the reliability of ratings or measures between individuals (for which statistical methods are available) and/or by using external, more objective, methods of rating.

◘ Using questionnaires as the only research method limits the reliability of findings.

Using other methods such as interviewing, or more extensive use of free text (even within a questionnaire), would improve the depth and breadth of information sought.

Measures of performance used and the

source of the evidence

Thirty-five performance dimensions were used in the empirical papers; a figure that slightly exceeds the number of measures used to identify elements of HRM. Figure 7 shows the 10 most frequently used performance measures and the percentages of studies that use those measures.

Thirty seven papers used an overall, or composite, measure of organisational/financial performance which was often derived from a number of variables.

Once again, there is a diversity of the performance measures used: no single measure dominates the analysis.

Forty-nine studies used the same source to measure performance and HRM practice/policy. Again, the most common type of measure was questionnaire, and the source of information was often the HR or another senior manager. Similar points should be noted as for elements of HRM in the previous section.

A larger number of studies used objective sources

Figure 8 | Measures of performance used in the empirical papers

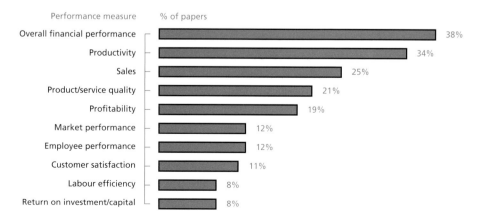

Performance measure	% of papers
Overall financial performance	38%
Productivity	34%
Sales	25%
Product/service quality	21%
Profitability	19%
Market performance	12%
Employee performance	12%
Customer satisfaction	11%
Labour efficiency	8%
Return on investment/capital	8%

such as databases and financial reports (n = 27) than for the elements of HRM. Although this amounts to under a third of the studies, it is possible to be more confident in these measures.

A recent commentary noted that many of the performance measures in the health sector are unique: clinical activity and workload (eg staff per occupied bed); outputs (eg number of patients treated) or outcome (eg mortality) (Buchan, 2004). Although four empirical papers were found which studied the health sector specifically, only one of them referred to any of these sector-specific measures – ie health outcomes – even though a health sector database was used.

This may be a result of the contested nature of performance indicators within the health sector, in the UK at least (see page 52). However, it may otherwise simply demonstrate the lack of empirical research in this area. It may also result from a search strategy that focuses on HRM and performance/productivity rather than specifically on 'health' or 'HR' outcomes (see page 31).

Context

The context of any empirical research – ie the situation in which the research was carried out – is important in speculating about the generalisability of findings. The industry in which the study was carried out is one aspect of context. Figure 9 shows that around half of the empirical papers were multi-industry studies.

Although multi-industry studies enable statements about generalisability of findings, the large data sets mean that

◻ they do not provide the opportunity to explore the context-specific contingencies such as strategy that differ across certain industries (Wright and Gardner, 2003)

◻ it is virtually impossible to study industry-specific measures of performance.

Those studies that have focused on a particular industry have primarily been carried out in manufacturing, telecommunications/IT and finance.

Figure 9 | The industrial context

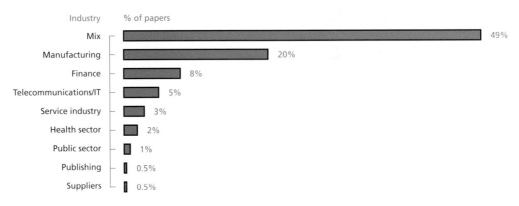

A second aspect of context is location. Figure 10 shows that the HRM–performance literature is predominantly based on research carried out in the USA and UK. Thirty-five studies were USA-based, and 24 UK-based (61 per cent of the total number of studies). Some writers argue that it is important to explore whether US-oriented models of the HRM–performance link are appropriate for other contexts (Boselie et al, 2003).

Research design

The research design – ie the way in which the data was gathered and analysed, indicates the extent to which causality may be determined between HRM and performance. To date the majority of empirical research in the HRM–performance literature has assumed that organisational performance is influenced by elements of HRM. However, there is an alternative interpretation. The 'reverse causation' hypothesis suggests that as firms perform better, they are more likely to invest in HRM (Wright and Gardener, 2003). Finding the direction of causality from existing empirical research is difficult because of research designs used.

Research designs, and the number of empirical papers which use each design, are shown in Table 9 on page 36.

- The majority of studies were cross-sectional in nature (n = 79, or 81 per cent). Cross-sectional studies are a cost-effective method of discovering whether two variables are associated in large data sets, which means that these papers may well have findings that are useful in other circumstances (Wall and Wood, 2005).

- There were also some quasi-longitudinal studies in the empirical papers.

Figure 10 | Country of study for HRM performance papers

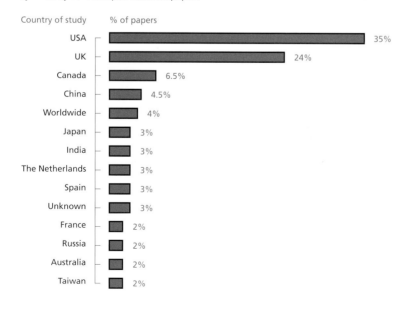

◘ Both cross-sectional and quasi-longitudinal studies support the proposition that there is an association between HRM and performance, but are unable to demonstrate *causal* evidence that HRM causes improved performance. This would only be achievable through longitudinal studies.

◘ Three studies had complete longitudinal design from which causal inferences about the relationships between HRM and performance could be made (Cappelli and Neumark, 2001; Ichniowski *et al*, 1997; Murray and Gerhart, 1998).

Two meta analyses brought together the results of other studies; they did not report new empirical work:

◘ One focused on the moderators of the team–performance link, which shows how the impact of a HRM practice on performance is contingent on elements of the HRM practice itself (Svyantek *et al*, 1999).

◘ The second explored the impact of worker participation on productivity (Doucouliagos, 1995).

Two case studies set out to explore how employees conceptualise the link between HRM and performance and these give some insight into how HRM and performance might be linked. These were classified separately as quasi-longitudinal (Truss, 2001) and cross-sectional (McAdam and Crowe, 2004).

Table 9 | Research design used by the empirical papers

Design	When is data gathered using this design?	What can this design show about the relationship between HRM and performance?	Percentage of empirical papers using this design
Longitudinal	– HRM and performance measured at time 1 – HRM measured at time 2 – Performance measured at time 3	– Can demonstrate causal relationship between HRM and performance if change in HRM is associated with change in subsequent performance	3
Quasi-longitudinal	– Performance measured at time 1 – HRM and performance measured at time 2	– Helps rule out reverse causality (that prior performance is associated with greater use of HRM) – Because HRM only measured at time 2, it cannot determine whether any change in HRM causes change in performance	14
Cross-sectional	– HRM and performance measured once only (concurrent or not)	– Demonstrates associations between HRM and performance – not causal links	81
Meta analysis	– No data-gathering; this method brings together the results of other empirical studies	– Systematic collection of data from more than one study; combined and analysed using robust statistics	2

Taking account of external factors in research design

The extent to which conditions in the environment are measured and controlled when exploring the HRM–performance link is important. A number of papers indicate conditions in the environment that influence HRM and performance. For example:

◘ firms that are larger might be expected to have more well-developed HRM practices (Youndt *et al*, 1996)

◘ unionisation status is also thought to vary with the HRM resource system and have potential direct effects on performance (Arthur, 1994)

◘ the age of the establishment might influence the rate of adoption of HRM practices (Pil and MacDuffie, 1996).

In order to reduce the impact of these potential sources of influence it is important to include measures for these factors (controls) and account for them. This is especially important when using a cross-sectional research design. The majority of studies that used a cross-sectional design included some control variables in their analyses to reduce the possibility of spurious results.

The most common external factors (controls) found to be affecting HRM and performance are firm size, firm age, unionisation, industry, organisational type and organisational ownership.

Findings from the empirical studies

In this section findings from the empirical papers are presented:

◘ relationships between HRM and performance

◘ HRM and other external/organisational factors

◘ relationships between combinations of elements of HRM

◘ relationships between the HRM–performance link and 'black box' variables.

Relationships between HRM and performance

Both positive and negative associations (in terms of statistical significance) between HRM and performance were recorded. Non-significant associations were also found. All are summarised in Table 10 on page 38. Papers which explored bundles of elements of HRM found the most positive associations with performance.

Three elements of HRM which have been explored the most (in terms of numbers of papers) were:

• Training and development

• Pay and incentives

• Involvement and voice

These three also demonstrated the largest number of positive associations with performance.

In order to explore these associations in more detail, it is necessary to understand how 'performance' was defined.

Table 11 on page 40 shows the associations between elements of HRM and various performance measures.

◘ Association is shown as either positive or non-significant, where more than 50 per cent of the number of papers exploring this association shows this effect.

◘ Associations where there is only one paper in a category are also shown.

◘ Blank cells show that there the evidence was mixed/relatively evenly spread between the three categories of association.

◘ The column headed 'Main association' represents the association with the most papers relating to that element of HRM when all types of performance measure are considered, without breaking down the relationship between individual elements of HRM and performance measures.

Table 10 | Numbers of empirical papers showing types of association between elements of HRM and performance

Element of HRM	Type of association			Main association between this element and performance[1]	Total number of papers exploring this association
	Positive	Negative	Non-signifiant		
Training/development	24	1	19	Positive	44
Pay/incentives[2]	21	6	20	Positive	47
Involvement/voice[3]	16	5	17	Non-significant	38
Selection/recruitment	7	4	12	Non-significant	23
Teamworking	7	0	7	Positive or non-significant	14
Performance appraisal	6	0	12	Non-significant	18
HR index/bundle	37	3	20	Positive	60
Security	0	0	2	Non-significant	2
Job design (including work–life balance)	8	1	12	Non-significant	21
Equal opportunities	1	0	2	Non-significant	3
Career development (including mentoring)	2	0	6	Non-significant	8

1 Defined as the type of association with the largest number of papers.
2 Including 'pay for performance'.
3 including 'information sharing/communication'.

Training and development is the most commonly studied element of HRM, and has a much higher number of positive associations with individual performance measures than any other single element, including organisational level performance measures such as productivity, firm performance and individual employee performance (see Figure 11).

Figure 11 | Significant positive, negative and non-significant associations between training and development and performance

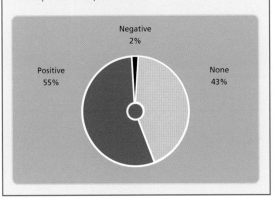

The evidence on the impact of pay and incentives is mixed, despite the relatively large number of studies with no dominant associations in any category (see Figure 12).

Figure 12 | Significant positive, negative and non-significant associations between pay and performance

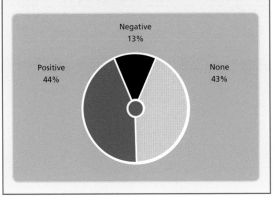

Involvement/voice and teamworking have positive associations with individual employee performance but not with any organisational-level performance measures (see Figure 13).

Figure 13 | Significant positive, negative and non-significant associations between involvement/voice and performance

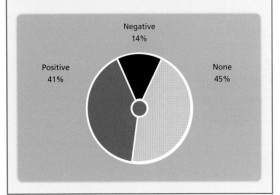

Bundles of HRM elements have positive associations with all organisational-level performance measures apart from market performance (see Figure 14).

Figure 14 | Significant positive, negative and non-significant associations between bundles of HRM and performance

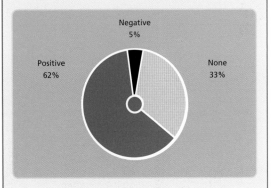

There are no elements of HRM which are mainly associated in a negative way with performance measures, although there are a number where the main association is not statistically significant.

Three elements of HRM that are not associated significantly with any performance measure:

- Recruitment and selection
- Performance appraisal
- Job design (including work–life balance)

Table 11 | Positive and non-significant associations between elements of HRM and performance measures

Performance / HRM	Financial performance[1]	Firm performance	Productivity	Sales	Quality[2]	Market performance	Employee performance	Efficiency	Main association between this element and performance	Total number of papers considering this association
Training/development	Not sig.	Positive	Positive	Not sig.	Positive	Positive	Positive	[1 only]	Positive	44
Pay / incentives	Not sig.	Not sig.				Not sig.		Not sig.	Positive	47
Involvement/ voice	Not sig.	Not sig.	Not sig.	[1 only]	[0]	Not sig.	Positive		Non-significant	38
Selection/ Recruitment	Not sig.	Not sig.	Not sig.	[1 only]	Not sig.	Not sig.	[1 only]	[0]	Non-significant	23
Teamworking	Not sig.	Not sig.		[1 only]		[0]	Positive	[1 only]	Positive or non-significant	14
Performance appraisal	Not sig.	Not sig.	Not sig.	[1 only]	Not sig.	[1 only]		[0]	Non-significant	18
HR index/ bundle	Positive	Positive	Positive	Positive	Positive		Positive	Positive	Positive	60
Security	[1 only]	[0]	[1 only]	[0]	[0]	[0]	[0]	[0]	Non-significant	2
Job design (including work-life balance)		Not sig.	Not sig.		Not sig.		[1 only]	[0]	Non-significant	21
Equal opportunities	[0]	[0]	Not sig.	[0]	[0]	[0]	[0]	[0]	Non-significant	3
Career development (including mentoring)	[1 only]	Not sig.	[1 only]	[0]	[1 only]	[1 only]	Not sig.	[0]	Non-significant	8

1 including 'profitability' and 'return on investment'
2 including 'customer satisfaction'

Table 12 | Significant associations between organisational factors and the HRM–performance link (figures represent the number of significant associations)

Organisational factor HRM–performance link (element of HRM involved)	Strategy	% professional/ ethnic/ disabled	HR IT	HR involvement	Climate	Location of firm	Size/age of firm	Industrial growth, capital, differentiation	Type of firm
Training	1 (a)				2 (b)				
Pay / incentives									2
Involvement / voice									1 (c)
Recruitment and selection			2 (f)	2 (f)	3				
Teamworking	2 (d)								
Performance appraisal	2 (a)								
Bundles	9				1	1	1	3	
Security									
Job design (including work–life balance)		2					1		
Equal opportunities		3							
Career development (including mentoring)									

The HRM–performance link and organisational characteristics

It was possible to determine significant associations between the HRM–performance link and organisational factors such as firm size and age, as well as internal factors such as the presence of a strategy, or the use of IT within the HR function (see Table 12 on page 41).

Sixteen papers found significant associations between organisational factors and the HRM–performance link. It is not possible to detail here all the relationships but some examples of the more commonly studied elements of HRM are given below (and cross-referenced in Table 12).

(a) Training and performance appraisal were associated with higher employee productivity where there was a differentiation strategy (Chang and Chen, 2002).

   – This was indicated by the importance of new product development, brand identification, innovation in product and service, innovation in marketing techniques and forecasting market growth.

(b) The strength of the relationship between professional development and sales/overall performance was altered by the work climate (Gelade and Ivery, 2003).

(c) The relationship between profit-sharing and ownership, and worker participation and productivity was stronger in labour-managed firms than in participatory capitalist firms (Doucouliagos, 1995).

(d) Teamworking was associated with higher employee productivity where there was a cost-focused strategy (Chang and Chen, 2002) or a differentiation strategy (see (a)).

   – A cost-focused strategy was indicated by the importance of operation efficiency, competitive pricing, procurement of raw materials, increasing capacity utilisation, the decreased number of product features and reducing product costs.

(e) Performance appraisal was more strongly associated with return on equity in firms with an innovation strategy (Delery and Doty 1996).

   – Innovation was indicated by being innovative in the way services are delivered, the offer of a wide variety of services, a diverse customer group, the number of new services offered, the novelty of new services offered, and the amount of resource allocated to marketing.

(f) Job analysis (as part of recruitment and selection) is positively related to financial performance and relative performance and is stronger in firms with HR information systems and HR involvement (Siddique, 2004).

– HR information systems were indicated by the number of in-house computerised systems, the range of information stored, and the number of applications.

– HR involvement was indicated by the ratio of HR staff to employees, the number of HR managers/directors in the company hierarchy, the proportion of corporate meetings that involve HR, the HR input to strategic decisions, and the importance top management accords to the HR function.

A large number of papers considered bundles of elements of HRM and performance. These are not detailed here (details are available on request from the authors).

The composition of the link between HRM and performance

Throughout this Report the link between HRM and performance is referred to as the 'black box'. There were three empirical papers which explored this link and provided evidence (see Table 13). In all cases there was an association between the element of HRM and the content of the 'black box' and then an association between the 'black box' and the performance measure.

These three papers demonstrate that it is possible to explore the 'black box' and to determine significant associations.

Any review of literature is limited, but it is nevertheless important to identify those limitations. Limitations of this review are shown in Appendix 1.

Table 13 | Significant associations between black box variables and the HRM–performance relationship

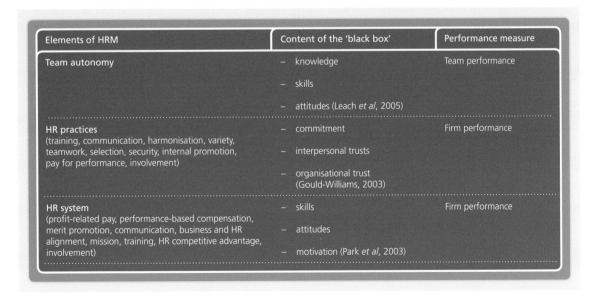

Elements of HRM	Content of the 'black box'	Performance measure
Team autonomy	– knowledge – skills – attitudes (Leach *et al*, 2005)	Team performance
HR practices (training, communication, harmonisation, variety, teamwork, selection, security, internal promotion, pay for performance, involvement)	– commitment – interpersonal trusts – organisational trust (Gould-Williams, 2003)	Firm performance
HR system (profit-related pay, performance-based compensation, merit promotion, communication, business and HR alignment, mission, training, HR competitive advantage, involvement)	– skills – attitudes – motivation (Park *et al*, 2003)	Firm performance

Summary

This chapter has reported on the review of empirical evidence for a relationship between HRM and performance. There are thousands of published papers exploring the links between HRM and performance (we found over 13,000).

However, 97 papers met the inclusion criteria. Conclusions have been drawn about both the papers themselves, and the empirical data which they present.

The empirical papers

Where did the data come from?

The majority of studies use one subjective data source, usually from the completion of a questionnaire, to gain information about HRM and performance. This means that some papers miss out on exploring the extent to which HRM is put into practice from the workers' or the line manager's perspective.

How objective was the data?

Over half of the papers used the same information source to rate HRM and organisational performance. It may be beneficial to use different sources for HRM and performance measures to overcome potential bias.

There was also relatively little use of objective data sources, although more were used to identify measures of performance than for elements of HRM.

Where were the studies carried out?

Over half of the papers had used multi-industry samples; where industry sectors were specified, these tended to be manufacturing, telecommunications/IT and finance. HRM–performance literature appears to be predominantly based on studies carried out in the USA and UK.

How were the studies carried out?

The majority of papers (up to 80 per cent) used cross-sectional samples with simple correlation or regression analysis. Although this enables studies to show that HRM is associated with performance, these papers cannot provide evidence that HRM causes changes in performance.

What was the theoretical basis for the research?

Most papers either did not state the theoretical perspective used, or appeared to use approaches from more than one perspective. It was not possible to classify the papers using theoretical frameworks.

Empirical data about HRM and performance

This review addressed questions about the HRM–performance relationship shown below.

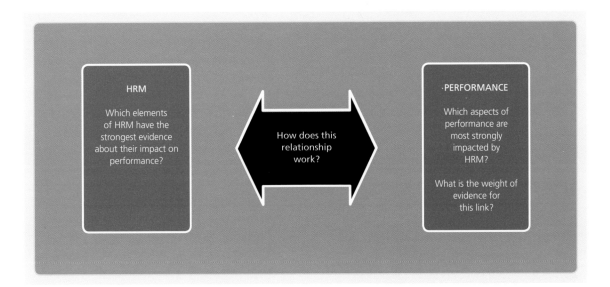

What is the weight of evidence for this link?

By definition, only papers which provided evidence about this link were analysed. This link is not always shown to be positive and it is often difficult to identify causality, and its direction, from the evidence available.

Which elements of HRM have the strongest evidence about their impact on performance?

Training, pay, involvement and bundles all featured as having the most significant and non-significant associations with performance but pay, involvement and bundles were also found to have the most negative associations with performance. There is insufficient evidence to suggest that any one element of HRM may be superior to another in terms of its impact on performance.

Over 30 different elements of HRM and performance measures were used in the papers. There was no single element of HRM that had been measured in all of the papers, or was dominant.

The most frequently studied measures of HRM in the papers were training and development, pay and employee involvement, and these also showed the largest number of positive associations with performance.

Training and development has the highest number of associations with individual performance measures including productivity, firm performance and employee performance.

The evidence on the links between pay and performance is very mixed, despite the relatively large number of studies.

This review does not find any significant associations between recruitment/selection, performance appraisal, job design and any individual performance measure.

Which aspects of performance are most strongly impacted by HRM?

Over 30 different performance measures were used in the papers. There was no single performance measure that had been measured in all of the papers, or was dominant.

The most popular performance measures in the papers were overall performance, productivity and sales. The largest number of positive associations with elements of HRM was with employee performance, all other organisational-level measures having the same number of associations.

How does this relationship work?

Relatively few papers explored the full link between HRM, black box and performance. Some reported that commitment, trust, skill, attitudes and motivation were important.

What is different about this review?

There have been a number of other reviews of some parts of the HRM–performance literature – eg Michie and Sheehan-Quinn, 2001; Boselie *et al*, 2005; Wall and Wood, 2005. However, this review is different in that

◘ it has examined a wider range of journals than previous reviews, and has included health journals in its focus

◘ it has focused on both single elements of HRM and bundles, whereas many previous reviews have focused mainly on bundles or HRM as a single entity

◘ it did not start with a predetermined framework for the relationship between HRM and performance but simply located all the relevant research and then identified the main research designs and underpinning theories.

4 | The NHS: strategy and performance

Key messages

◘ The NHS has produced a variety of policies to form a 'strategy'. Recent focus has been on a patient-centred and patient-led service.

◘ At the same time, the NHS has multiple stakeholders and a complex structure, which makes the implementation of performance management difficult. However, there is more performance data available than ever before.

◘ Performance measurement debates focus on what should be measured, and how, rather than whether performance should be measured at all.

◘ The NHS has a performance management framework designed to address some of the criticisms about assessment methodologies used prior to this time, and to attempt to make the measures more patient-focused. They are not, however, focused on clincial outcomes at the individual level.

The previous chapter illustrated the importance of aspects of context in determining links between HRM and performance. It also illustrated the importance of context-specific measures of performance.

This chapter describes the context of the research – the NHS. It also presents the organisational strategy and the methods by which its performance is currently assessed. In addition it highlights the role of HRM.

The core principles of the NHS

◘ The NHS will provide a universal service for all, based on clinical need, not ability to pay.

◘ The NHS will provide a comprehensive range of services.

◘ The NHS will shape its services around the needs and preferences of individual patients, their families and their carers.

◘ The NHS will respond to the different needs of different populations.

◘ The NHS will work continuously to improve quality services and to minimise errors.

◘ The NHS will support and value its staff.

◘ Public funds for health care will be devoted solely to NHS patients.

◘ The NHS will work together with others to ensure a seamless service for patients.

◘ The NHS will help to keep people healthy and work to reduce health inequalities.

The strategy of the NHS

The NHS does not have a single document termed a strategy – although many staff regard the *NHS Plan* and subsequent policies as the 'strategy' in that it has driven most of the changes in the NHS since 2000. Recent direction suggests that

the NHS is changing the way it works to make sure patients always come first.

(Department of Health, 2005d)

The core principles for the NHS were set out in the *NHS Plan*.

The NHS Plan

The *NHS Plan* is summarised as follows:

a plan for investment in the NHS with sustained increases in funding. This is a plan for reform with far-reaching changes across the NHS. The purpose and vision of this NHS Plan is to give the people of Britain a health service fit for the 21st century: a health service designed around the patient.

(Department of Health, 2000)

The *NHS Plan* contained targets for increased numbers of beds, staff and facilities. The *NHS Plan* homepage (Department of Health, 2005e) details the various documents produced subsequently which describe in more detail the implications of the *NHS Plan* for both staff and patients. Many functional areas have subsequently produced their own guides to the implementation of the *NHS Plan* in their area, including HR (Department of Health, 2002), which forms the HR strategy for the NHS.

The *NHS Improvement Plan*

This document was published in June 2004 (Department of Health, 2004c) and set out priorities until 2008. It built on the *NHS Plan*:

Less than four years into the period covered by the 10-year NHS Plan, the new delivery systems and providers are expanding capacity and choice. The foundations for success are now in place and it is time to move on.

In particular, there is reference to the achievement of waiting targets, so that waiting is not now seen as the key issue. The *NHS Improvement Plan* can be summarised as having two key aspects (see box below).

The NHS Improvement Plan

Offering a better service

- supporting people with long-term conditions
- a healthier and fitter population
- high-quality and personalised care.

Making it happen

- getting information to work for the patient
- more staff, working differently
- investment, new capacity, and diversity of provision
- aligning incentives with patients and professionals
- empowering local communities.

The role of the workforce

The role of staff in these improvements is described as not so much being about more staff but about how they work.

Greater flexibility and growth in the way services are provided will be matched by increases in NHS staff and new ways of working to meet patients' needs. By 2008 the number of staff working for the NHS will have increased significantly. Staff will be given more help to train and learn new skills … This flexible working to deliver more personalised and user-friendly care for patients will be rewarded by better pay for NHS staff.

There is significant emphasis on the role of staff in these changes, as it is argued that these changes will support staff in their work:

The changes set out in this document will mean, for the first time, that the system will work with and support those professional instincts of the NHS's dedicated staff and ensure high-quality personal care for patients. It will reward the NHS for these efforts, take away the barriers to doing the right thing and make it easier for dedicated doctors, nurses and thousands of other NHS staff to follow their calling to cure and to care … Excellence becomes the norm for clinical staff and managers alike.

The impact of this strategy on the workforce was summarised as a series of 'high-impact policy changes' (not to be confused with the ten 'High-Impact Changes', Department of Health, 2005b). These are shown in Table 14.

Table 14 | Policy impact on the workforce

Policy	Impact on workforce
Significant reductions in waiting times	Continuing growth in capacity, particularly workforce capacity
An expansion in the plurality of provision	Increasing numbers of NHS staff working in or alongside private sector staff
Choice and personalised care	NHS staff will be required to engage differently with every single patient
Policies on improving health and managing long-term conditions	Driving new roles for staff, and greater flexibility between primary and secondary care
Delivering the efficiency requirements from the Independent Review of Public Sector Efficiency (Gershon, 2004)	Improvements in efficiency and productivity – with the workforce providing the biggest element: half of all savings
The National Programme for IT (NpfIT)[1]	Fundamental change of the way staff work on a day-to-day basis, how they interact with patients and where they work
The implementation of changes to junior doctors' employment contracts (eg 48-hour week)	Major workforce redesign
A White Paper on public health (Department of Health, 2004c)	New roles and responsibilities are described to deliver high-quality health improvement services

1. Called 'Connecting for Health' from 1 April 2005

In addition, it is clear that there will be an emphasis on good HR management and a focus on ensuring that management costs remain proportionate to changes in the workforce (Department of Health, 2005f).

Improving public sector efficiency

The Gershon review of public sector efficiency (Gershon, 2004) led to the Productive Time programme (Department of Health, 2005g), which aims to make better use of staff time – not getting staff to work harder, but enabling staff to work smarter, spending more time on where it matters for them and for patients – ie high-quality direct-contact care.

Productive Time is expected to yield £3.8 billion yearly benefits by 2007/2008 against a 2003/2004 baseline. There are three key strategies within this programme, recognising the centrality of workforce in the implementation of the strategy:

- *process*: Ten High-Impact Changes (HIC)

- *people*: Workforce Reform

- *technology* : NHS Connecting for Health.

Elements affecting the workforce are detailed as (Department of Health, 2005g):

- new roles and skill-mix, resulting in

a lower net cost, increased output and/or improved quality (eg reduced treatment delay)

- enhancement of

the roles of professionals and support staff

in order to

release clinicians' time to increase their output and maximise patient contact time.

- This approach is also expected to increase job satisfaction as work becomes more challenging and interesting and allows staff

the opportunity to utilise their skills more effectively.

- managing overhead costs by improving staff retention:

It is estimated that a reduction of turnover by 1 per cent to 13 per cent would result in annualised savings of £90 million by 2007/2008.

Many organisations are also using an increasing evidence base to develop progressive people management policy such as increased teamworking and staff involvement, which reduce stress, turnover and sickness absence and improve patient care.

- by reducing temporary staff and agency costs:

Improved retention should reduce the need for temporary staff. Empirical evidence shows that replacing temporary staff with experienced permanent staff also leads to increased productivity and better-quality patient care.

- by improving sickness management

- and by e-recruitment.

HR in the NHS

We are moving on from a 'top-down' target-driven management system to one which has the right incentives to make sure that we respond to patients and continually improve… giving patients more choices, giving the people who are often the closest to them – GPs – more power, giving provider organisations more freedoms to respond, making sure the money follows the patient and introducing more transparent standard setting and inspection.

(Department of Health, 2005h)

The importance of the workforce has been described as:

◘ valuing NHS staff for the benefit of patients

Our patients and users will only feel truly valued and cared for if our staff feel truly valued and cared for as well … But far too many of our staff feel they're doing a good job despite rather than with the help of managers and reforms. Too many feel that change is being inflicted upon them instead of happening with them. It's no wonder that stress is even more of an occupational hazard in the NHS than in many other large organisations.

◘ engaging clinicians and transforming staff

We need to engage the people of the NHS – particularly our clinicians – in shaping and making the change: and we need to give them the support so that they can fulfil their potential … That's what we're doing with Agenda for Change – not another technical reform but one of the most radical frameworks for transformation that we negotiated with our staff and their unions.

HR professionals are crucial:

Your role in HR is so vital. You are the glue in the system. You can provide the leadership, the

inspiration and the support that we need to deliver the world-class service that patients want and deserve – you are the ones who can really help make it happen.

(Department of Health, 2005i)

Performance management[1]

In the market for new management ideas … performance management has been one of the success stories of the past decade.

(Smith, 2002)

There is more performance data available on the NHS than ever before. Performance management is not unique to health care, or even to the public sector, with the equivalent of one new article on business performance measurement appearing every five hours of every working day in the mid-1990s (Neely, 1999).

Financial measures have long been used to evaluate performance in commercial organisations, although criticism of performance measures derived from costing and accounting systems began to gain credence in the 1970s (Bourne *et al*, 2000). By the early 1980s there was a growing realisation that it was no longer appropriate to use financial measures as the sole criteria for assessing organisational success (Kennerley and Neely, 2002).

A number of performance measurement models and frameworks have been developed in order to measure private sector performance and overcome the shortcomings associated with purely financial measurement systems:

◘ the SMART pyramid
  (Cross and Lynch, 1988/1999)

- the performance measurement matrix (Keegan *et al*, 1989)

- the results and determinants matrix (Fitzgerald *et al*, 1991)

- the balanced scorecard (Kaplan and Norton, 1992)

- the performance prism (Neely *et al*, 2002).

However, the adoption of such private sector performance management models by the public sector has been viewed with some scepticism (Boyne, 1996; Parker and Subramaniam, 1964; Ranson and Stewart, 1994).There are a number of reasons for this:

- Sayre (1953) stated that public and private organisations are

fundamentally alike in all unimportant respects.

- Allison (1979) argues further that

the notion that there is any significant body of private management practices and skills that can be transferred directly to public management tasks in a way that produces significant improvements is wrong.

- Moriarty and Kennedy (2002) added that

because public sector service organisations operate without market competition, the implementation of performance measurement is often used as a substitute for market pressures.

- However, Glynn and Murphy (1996) discuss performance in terms of accountability, stating:

there is a need to develop quantitative measures that can assess the efficiency and effectiveness of policy and its implementation.

The implementation of 'private sector' performance measurement frameworks within public sector organisations has been studied. Examples include: balanced scorecard implementation (Radnor and McGuire, 2004; Chan, 2004), EFQM implementation (Moullin, 2002; Eskildsen et al, 2004; Wisniewski and Stewart, 2004), and the performance prism (Neely *et al*, 2002). Most public organisations do not have the same strategic freedom that private companies have because some of their strategic goals are decided by politicians (Lane, 1993).

The role of stakeholders from a performance measurement perspective has been little discussed. The issue of who is seen as the end user of the performance measurement information generated has received little attention and yet, particularly in the public sector, is of critical importance.

(Wisniewski and Stewart, 2004)

It has been argued that having multiple stakeholders often results in the use of performance measurement as merely a diagnostic tool rather than an interactive one within public sector organisations (Radnor and McGuire, 2004; Osborne *et al*, 1995).

Performance management in the NHS

Performance management within the NHS has been defined as a

set of managerial instruments designed to secure optional performance of the health care system over time, in line with policy objectives.

(Smith, 2002)

Performance management consists of:

☐ *guidance* (to transmit policy objectives)

☐ *monitoring* (collecting and analysing information)

☐ *response* (to stimulate appropriate remedial actions and promote continuous improvement) (Smith, 2002).

Such 'consciously active management of strategic organisational behaviour is largely untested in health care' (Smith, 2002), in that most previous systems have relied on the micro-management of clinical behaviour or passive systems of regulation to deliver improvement. A large review of the performance frameworks for health systems in the UK, Canada, Australia, the USA, including the World Health Organisation (WHO) and the Organisation for Economic Co-operation and Development (OECD) concluded all the frameworks differed in both concept and operation, the indicators being mainly concerned with outcome rather than process and the drive being improving health and managing the health system around the consumer (Arah *et al*, 2003).

There are many other stakeholders of the NHS who may influence performance measurement. These may include (Appleby *et al*, 2002) the stakeholders of the NHS:

☐ *funders* – taxpayers

☐ *the Government* – Treasury, ministers, parliament, local government

☐ *health professionals* – clinicians, Royal Colleges, RCN, BMA, etc

☐ *management* – NHS managers, SHAs

☐ *media* – broadcast, print, Internet

☐ *private and voluntary sectors* – pharmaceutical industry, NHS suppliers, voluntary organisations

☐ *regulators* – Audit Commission, National Audit Office

☐ *researchers* – academics, consultants

☐ *users* – patients, carers.

These groups differ in the level of aggregation of performance data that they require, as well as the type of data. It is argued, therefore, that any performance measurement system must be multi-levelled and flexible so as to be able to capture different views on 'what matters'.

Levels of performance are also important when performance data is aggregated – many performance indicators cannot be 'added up' to form the basis of judgement about overall performance of a system, because of inherent trade-offs between different aspects of a system – eg access time and quality of care. Very often neither the relationship between various performance measures is discussed, nor the basis for the sampling of measures justified (Appleby *et al*, 2002).

Telling the public about performance

This subject continues to receive high-profile media attention with an emphasis on developing measures that can be easily understood by the public, in line with the policy emphasis on a patient-led NHS (Department of Health, 2005d). There is also an ongoing debate about public

'There has been particular focus on patients' health-related quality of life as a potentially useful outcome measure ...'

disclosure of performance results (Shaw, 2003; Mannion and Davies, 2002) which is seen as not always leading to performance improvement, but which may be a key factor for the introduction of patient choice within the NHS.

What is measured?

Whereas many would agree that outcome measures should be the focus of attention within health care, it is clear that managerial attempts to improve performance often focus on the process of care (Davies *et al*, 2002). The case for using outcome measures is that:

◘ patients are most interested in outcomes, and so a performance system which focuses on them will encourage professional attention towards the patient

◘ outcome data is needed to determine 'what works', and measures of outcome (eg mortality) are generic and long-term in nature

◘ a focus on outcomes can encourage innovation

◘ many outcome measures are free from manipulation by providers of care, whereas process measures can induce dysfunctional behaviour.

There has been particular focus on patients' health-related quality of life (HRQoL) as a potentially useful outcome measure (Appleby and Devlin, 2005), as the focus on improving patients' quality of life has become a clear goal for the NHS (Department of Health, 2000). It is now being argued that the advent of patient choice (Appleby *et al*, 2003) and the mechanism of payment by results (PbR) will mean that both commissioners and patients need better information about the

outcome of the processes they are commissioning or choosing (Meikle, 2005; Appleby and Devlin, 2005).

However, there is also a case for process measures:

◘ Some aspects of process (eg access speed) are valued by patients, independent of outcome.

◘ There may be no consensus about what constitutes outcome, or even if there is, there may be no consensus about how to measure the outcome (eg when should death after surgery be measured?), and collecting the data may be very costly.

◘ Process measures are almost instantaneous and can be acted on quickly, whereas outcomes are often evident only after a long time period.

◘ Process measures are usually attributable to the provider of care, whereas outcome measures may be influenced by a much wider range of factors and may be subject to more random variation. Certain aspects of process are associated with desired outcomes.

◘ Incentive schemes can be more easily designed to relate to process measures than outcomes, and poor performance on a process measure gives clearer indication of the remedial action required.

The decision over whether to focus on process or outcomes therefore depends on the context, and this is an ongoing debate within healthcare (Crombie and Davies, 1998). Some argue that

the issue is not primarily one of whether to use process or outcome indicators, but rather how best to employ both in a way that is cognisant

'The NHS itself is not the only source of performance data ...'

*of the advantages and disadvantages of each
and relates their use and interpretation to these
characteristics.*

(Thomson, 2002)

How many measures are needed?

There has also been considerable debate about the
number of performance measures used within the
NHS, and whether it may be possible to develop
a single composite indicator of performance in
order to indicate overall performance (Appleby and
Mulligan, 2000).

Another facet of the debate is the extent to
which 'soft' information is used in performance
assessment (Goddard *et al*, 1999), although the
definition of these two types of information is
problematic, and is perhaps better viewed as
two extremes on a continuum. However, a crude
definition could regard 'soft' information as
subjective and qualitative and 'hard' as objective
and quantitative (Goddard *et al*, 1999), with
this distinction within the NHS leading to the
conclusion that 'hard' data is often produced
from formal performance assessment mechanisms
whereas 'soft' data is transmitted through informal
networks and mechanisms, and may be more
private.

The conclusions drawn by Goddard *et al*, (1999)
are that although hard data is used to assess
performance at the organisational level, this is
usually supplemented with soft data, and that
the hard data is used as a 'safety net' to locate
exceptional cases rather than as a positive sign of
good performance.

Is more data needed – or just 'better' data?

There is a case for needing more and/or
'better' data in order to be able to assess NHS
performance (Smith, 2003). Some substantial
research studies have come to similar conclusions
(Leatherman and Sutherland, 2003), citing a lack
of common understanding of the 'state of quality'.

The recent Chief Executive's report on the state
of the NHS makes a similar point, and describes
the need for measures of output and outcome
extending beyond hospitals (Department of
Health, 2004d).

However, others are proposing that there is more
that can be done with the current data (Lakhani *et
al*, 2005), an argument that may be valid given the
proliferation of performance data in the past 10
years (Nutley and Smith, 1998).

How is it measured?

Various methods can be used for performance
measurement including regulatory inspection,
patient/public surveys, third-party assessments,
statistical indicators and internal inspections
(Shaw, 2003). The NHS itself is not the only source
of performance data – organisations such as dr
foster[2] (an independent organisation providing
information about the quality and availability of
health services) collect and make available a wide
range of information. The Healthcare Commission
also carries out regular patient and staff surveys
which provide substantial data.

The NHS performance framework until 2005

The system used up to and including 2004/2005 (ending 31 March 2005) was one of 'star ratings', using a set of key indicators and a 'balanced scorecard' of some 30 others. For 2004/2005 the key targets for acute trusts were:

◘ maximum 12-hour waits for emergency admission via A&E post decision to admit

◘ all cancers: maximum two-week wait

◘ elective patients to wait longer than the standard

◘ financial management

◘ hospital cleanliness

◘ outpatient and elective (inpatient and daycase) booking

◘ outpatients to wait longer than the standard

◘ total time in A&E to be four hours or less.

The description of this system is included here because it is to be used as the basis for a selection of case-study sites for the second phase of the research. The ratings system is summarised in Table 15.

It should be noted that none of the key targets is directly workforce-related although one of the balanced scorecard indicators for acute trusts was 'workforce', described as:

The NHS will be transformed through implementing modern employment practices under the umbrella of the Improving Working Lives *standard, leading to improvements in the working lives of staff, and improvements in retention and recruitment. Furthermore, maintaining a healthy workforce is vital to delivering the best results for patients and maintaining workforce numbers.*

The NHS performance framework 'workforce' indicator

◘ *Improving Working Lives* – an assessment made by the SHA of progress towards 'practice plus' level (not compulsory for Foundation Trusts)

Table 15 | NHS performance ('star') ratings

The NHS performance ratings system placed NHS Trusts in England in one of four categories:

1 Trusts with the highest levels of performance are awarded a performance rating of three stars

2 Trusts that are performing well overall, but have not quite reached the same consistently high standards, are awarded a performance rating of two stars

3 Trusts where there is some cause for concern regarding particular areas of performance are awarded a performance rating of one star

4 Trusts that have shown the poorest levels of performance against the indicators or have been assessed to have significant areas of weakness for clinical governance are awarded a performance rating of zero stars. A zero star Trust is one which either fails against the key targets or is considered to have significant areas of weakness for clinical governance.

Where a trust has a low rating based on poor performance on a number of key targets and indicators, this does not necessarily mean that a hospital is unsafe, does not contain some very good clinical services or that the staff are not working hard in often difficult circumstances. It does mean that performance must be improved in a number of key areas.

◘ sickness absence rate – the amount of time lost through absence as a percentage of staff time available. This does not cover maternity leave, carer's leave or any periods of absence agreed under family-friendly/flexible working policies

◘ junior doctors' hours – the number of junior doctors complying in full with the New Deal on junior doctors' hours as a percentage of the number of junior doctors in post.

The scores for the three elements above were combined to form an overall score for the indicator (details for 2005/2006 not available at the time of writing).

Results from three elements of the staff survey are also included in the balanced scorecard:

◘ health, safety and incidents – assessed by views on work-related injury/illness, physical violence, harassment, bullying and abuse

◘ HRM – assessed by views on appraisals, personal development plans, access to training and development and teamworking

◘ staff attitudes – assessed by job satisfaction, intention to leave.

From now on

The performance of NHS organisations is now assessed by the Healthcare Commission (The Healthcare Commission, 2005a), the successor to the Commission for Healthcare Improvement (CHI), set up to

promote and drive improvement in the quality of health care and public health by becoming an authoritative and trusted source of information and by ensuring that this information is used to drive improvement

formed by the Health and Social Care (Community Health and Standards) Act 2003, and launched on 1 April 2004. Its role is described in the box below.

Statutory duties of the Healthcare Commission (in England)

◘ to assess the management, provision and quality of NHS health care and public health services

◘ to review the performance of each NHS Trust and award an annual performance rating

◘ to regulate the independent health care sector through registration, annual inspection, monitoring complaints and enforcement

◘ to publish information about the state of health care

◘ to consider complaints about NHS organisations that the organisations themselves have not resolved

◘ to promote the coordination of reviews and assessments carried out by ourselves and others to carry out investigations of serious failures in the provision of health care.

The Commission's assessments will be based around the concept of an 'annual health check' (The Healthcare Commission, 2005b), the components of which are shown in Figure 15. This approach has been summarised by the Chief Executive of the Healthcare Commission as

a new annual health check comprising standards and targets. The aim is to offer a richer picture of performance in a less burdensome way.

(Anon, 2005)

As can be seen, there are two components to the annual review:

◘ core standards that all NHS organisations in England should be achieving now – is the organisation getting the basics right?

◘ developmental standards that they should be aiming to achieve in the future – Is the organisation making and sustaining progress?

Their ratings and inspections will be carried out using agreed frameworks.

Core standards – getting the basics right

The 'core standards' aspect of the latest framework is based on *Standards for Better Health* (Department of Health, 2004e) and comprises seven domains (see Table 16), each with associated core and developmental standards.

◘ 'Existing targets' refer to the 20 targets to which the NHS is already committed from the *NHS Plan*, which are mostly concerned with access and relate to the key targets in the previous performance framework. The same methods of assessment will be used.

◘ 'Use of resources' examines financial performance and how well money is spent. This will be determined using results from the work of the Audit Commission and Monitor.

Figure 15 | The 'annual health check'

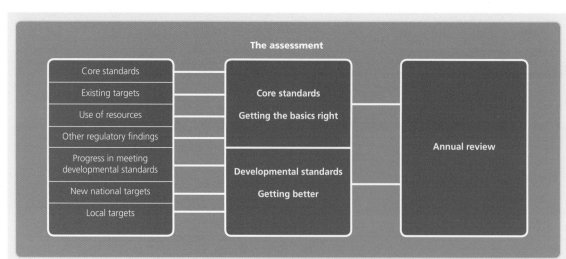

Developmental standards – getting better

◘ For 'getting better' there will be more detail developed during 2005/2006, but at present it is anticipated that this will be assessed using improvement reviews focusing on an aspect of the patients' pathway: a service – eg adult community mental health – a population group – eg children – and/or a condition – eg heart failure. These reviews will also focus on one domain of the developmental standards. Any new national targets will also be included in this aspect of the performance assessment.

From 2005/2006 the Healthcare Commission is intending to assess all NHS organisations in England, initially focusing on the core standards and subject to further legislation.

From 2006/2007 it plans to assess independent healthcare organisations by reference to the same core and developmental standards. The annual performance rating for all NHS organisations (essentially replacing the 'star ratings') will be in two parts (see Table 17 on page 60).

Table 16 | *Standards for Better Health*

Domain	Outcome
First Domain – Safety	Patient safety is enhanced by the use of health care processes, working practices and systemic activities that prevent or reduce the risk of harm to patients
Second Domain – Clinical and cost-effectiveness	Patients achieve health care benefits that meet their individual needs through health care decisions and services, based on what assessed research evidence has shown provides effective clinical outcomes
Third Domain – Governance	Managerial and clinical leadership and accountability, as well as the organisation's culture, systems and working practices, ensure that probity, quality assurance, quality improvement and patient safety are central components of all activities of the health care organisation
Fourth Domain – Patient focus	Health care is provided in partnership with patients, their carers and relatives, respecting their diverse needs, preferences and choices, and in partnership with other organisations (especially social care organisations) whose services impact on patient well-being
Fifth Domain – Accessible and responsive care	Patients receive services as promptly as possible, have choice in access to services and treatments, and do not experience unnecessary delay at any stage of service delivery or of the care pathway
Sixth Domain – Care environment and amenities	Care is provided in environments that promote patient and staff well-being and respect for patients' needs and preferences in that they are designed for the effective and safe delivery of treatment, care or a specific function, provide as much privacy as possible, are well maintained and are cleaned to optimise health outcomes for patients
Seventh Domain – Public health	Programmes and services are designed and delivered in collaboration with all relevant organisations and communities to promote, protect and improve the health of the population served and reduce health inequalities between different population groups and areas

The Healthcare Commission explains what it means by the use of the term 'staff' in its definitions of standards:

This term refers to everyone delivering NHS services… The health care organisation should consider, where relevant, their arrangements for the following groups:
- *employed staff*
- *independent contractors and their staff*
- *other contractors*
- *staff on honorary contracts*
- *staff seconded from other transitions*
- *locum, temporary and agency staff*
- *volunteers.*

(Healthcare Commission, 2005c)

The domains where workforce issues are specifically referred to are shown in Table 18.

However, there are also a number of other standards where the term 'staff' is used or part of the workforce referred to, mainly in relation to other activities which impact on staff (see Table 19 on page 62).

The impact of performance management in the NHS

There are a number of reviews of the performance system in the NHS to date (Smith, 2002; Appleby *et al*, 2002). One critique of performance measurement systems was provided by Appleby *et al* (2002) who concluded that:

The present set of performance indicators reflects the accidents of history and convenience rather than a systematic attempt to capture the various viewpoints which have an interest in NHS performance.

The views of some are that without the targets that have been in place, hospital performance (especially around waiting times) would not have improved so dramatically. However, it has also been suggested that targets may compromise other aspects of the service, and it is the associated rewards and sanctions that actually drive improvement, rather than the targets themselves.

Table 17 | New organisational ratings

Core standards and existing targets will have a combined rating of	An overall organisational rating will include assessment of the use of resources, new national targets and the results of improvement reviews, and will be
◘ Fully met	◘ Excellent
◘ Almost met	◘ Good
◘ Partly met	◘ Fair
◘ Not met	◘ Weak

Within the NHS a variety of incentives could address the perspectives of differing staff groups at all levels and may operate at individual or group/organisation level. Incentives within the NHS have traditionally been very mixed and often piecemeal and/or contradictory and weak (where exhortations to improve performance are not backed up with sanctions). Much recent NHS policy around the workforce – including the Consultant Contract, the new GP contracts and *Agenda for Change* – is seeking to provide new incentives for performance improvement at an individual and professional group level.

There is evidence to suggest that many managers and clinicians were not happy with the performance regime (Greener, 2005), regarding it as not measuring the important things:

endemic problems in … organisations were not dealt with because they were not being picked up by the … performance measures.

Table 18 | Workforce references in *Standards for Better Health*

Third Domain – Governance
Core standards
C8 Healthcare organisations *support their staff* through:
C8a having access to processes which permit them to raise, in confidence and without prejudicing their position, concerns over any aspect of service delivery, treatment or management that they consider to have an detrimental effect on patient care or on the delivery of services
C8b organisational and personal development programmes which *recognise the contribution and value of staff*, and address, where appropriate, under-representation of minority groups
C10 Health care organisations:
C10a undertake appropriate employment checks and *ensure that all employed or contracted professionally qualified staff are registered* with the appropriate bodies
C10b require that *all employed professionals abide by relevant published codes of professional practice*
C11 Health care organisations ensure that staff concerned with all aspects of the provision of health care:
C11a *are appropriately recruited, trained and qualified* for the work they undertake
C11b *participate in mandatory training programmes*
C11c *participate in further professional and occupational development* commensurate with their work throughout their working lives
Developmental standards
D5 Health care organisations work together and with social care organisations to meet the changing needs of their population by:
D5a *having an appropriately constituted workforce* with appropriate skill mix across the community
D5b ensuring the continuous improvement of services through *better ways of working*
D7 Health care organisations work to enhance patient care by *adopting best practice in human resources management and continually improving staff satisfaction*

Table 19 | Other references to 'staff'

First Domain – Safety

Core standards

C4   Healthcare organisations *keep patients, staff and visitors safe* by having systems to ensure that:

    C4e   the prevention, segregation, handling, transport and disposal of waste is properly managed so as to *minimise the risks to the health and safety of staff*, patients, the public and the safety of the environment

Developmental standards

D1   Health care organisations continuously and systematically review and improve all aspects of their activities that directly affect patient safety and *apply best practice in assessing and managing risks to patients, staff and others*, particularly when patients move from the care of one organisation to another

Second Domain – Clinical and cost-effectiveness

Core standards

Health care organisations ensure that

    C5b   *clinical care and treatment are carried out under supervision and leadership*

    C5c   *clinicians continuously update skills and techniques relevant to their clinical work*

Third Domain – Governance

Core standards

Health care organisations

    C7b   *actively support employees* to promote openness, honesty, probity, accountability, and the economic, efficient and effective use of resources

Developmental standards

Health care organisations work together to

    D4c   *ensure effective clinical and managerial leadership and accountability*

Fourth Domain – Patient focus

Core standards

C13 Health care organisations have systems in place to ensure that:

    C13a   *staff treat patients, their relatives and carers with dignity and respect*

    C13c   *staff treat patient information confidentially*, expect where authorised by legislation to the contrary

Sixth Domain – Care environment and amenities

Core standards

C20   Health care services are provided in environments which promote effective care and optimise health outcomes by being

    C20a   *a safe and secure environment which protects* patients, *staff*, visitors and their property, and the physical assets of the organisation

Developmental standards

D12   Health care is provided in well-designed environments that

    D12a   *promote* patient and *staff well-being*, and meet patients' needs and preferences, and *staff concerns*

Greener argues that 'gaming' resulting from the performance framework may have led to less attention on patient care.

Criticism has therefore been levelled at both the use of performance targets (the process) and the content of the targets themselves (are they measuring the 'right' things?). Smith (2002) noted that if performance management of this type were to be effective in the NHS it would require alignment of various priorities, adequate capacity for the performance management process and the engagement of clinicians (Morgan, 2005). Neely *et al* (2002) warn that performance measurement is merely a means to an end and go on to state:

Measures provide data which allow progress to be assessed. They do not, and never will, ensure that progress is made.

Endnotes

1   Thanks to Claire Moxham from Manchester Business School for much of the background research used in this section

2   www.drfoster.co.uk

5 | Consultations

Key messages

◘ The consultations showed that NHS staff share common values, whether they work at the front line providing services or work in management within the organisation. Both HRM staff and clinicians derived their motivation from feeling that they made a difference to the local community through the provision of health care.

◘ The impact of the NHS Plan on the NHS workforce has been articulated through the development of a variety of HRM policies, focused on making the NHS a model employer, ensuring that the NHS provides a model career through offering a Skills Escalator, improving staff morale and building people management skills.

◘ No unitary approach to HRM was identified in the consultations. Systems of HRM and interventions were highly context-specific and contingent upon other organisational factors, such as structural arrangements recognising HR at Board level or delegation of this responsibility to another Board member.

◘ The division of responsibility for people management between HR managers and line managers was a source of conflict. Line managers recognised the expertise of HR managers which they lacked, but if people management processes such as disciplinary procedures and recruitment are to be successfully devolved, line managers need additional support.

◘ The HR function is concerned with a number of areas of activity: recruitment and retention, pay and rewards, communication and teamworking.

◘ Although Trust performance is assessed through a range of performance indicators and targets, few links have been made between HR practices and performance outcomes within individual Trusts. There is one workforce indicator within the old performance framework which was seen as having recognised the contribution of HR to organisational performance.

This chapter describes the process and outcomes of consultations involving seven meetings held between January and April 2005, and forms an adjunct to the concurrent systematic review of literature relating HRM to performance.

The specific purpose of the consultation meetings was to gain views from a wide range of HR practitioners and clinical staff about how HRM contributes to performance in the NHS. The discussion in the meetings was focused around three questions:

◘ What is human resource management?

◘ What are the key issues you face at work in relation to HRM, and how should they be addressed?

'The ... purpose of the consultation meetings was to gain views from a wide range of HR practitioners and clinical staff ...'

- What works and what does not work in terms of HR practices?

However, we have analysed the data gathered and present it here in a format which enables comparison with findings from other data sources covered in this report, rather than simply listing the responses to the questions above.

A variety of perspectives emerged at the consultations. There was some disagreement amongst participants both about the nature of the issues and their potential solutions. For this reason the contents of each section appear at times to be contradictory – but this illustrates the nature of the issues under discussion.

Table 20 | Participants in the consultation meetings

Organisational background	NHS (49)	Non-NHS (11)
NHS staff responsibilities	HR professionals (34) including	
	▪ Directors of HR (17)	
	▪ Heads of HR or HR managers (17)	
	Non-HR (15) including	
	▪ Directors 5 (clinical 2, operational 3)	
	▪ Heads of service or managers 10 (clinical 4, operational 6)	
Organisations represented	▪ Department of Health (6)	Private and other sectors including
	▪ Strategic Health Authorities including Workforce development function (3)	▪ Private health care (2)
	▪ Acute Trusts (16)	▪ Hospitality industry (1)
	▪ Primary Care Trusts (15)	▪ IT industry (2)
	▪ Mental Health and Social Care Trusts (5)	▪ HR professional body (2)
	▪ Ambulance Trusts (2)	▪ Charity (1)
	▪ NHS Direct (1) (NHS organisation data missing for 2 participants)	▪ Union and arbitration (2)
Countries represented	England (55) Scotland (1) Wales (1) Roles which have international coverage (3)	

Participation

Sixty participants attended group meetings: details of their background are given in Table 20. Participants were able to comment on a draft version of this chapter in order to verify and modify reporting to represent content more accurately.

The HR function in the NHS

There was considerable debate about the HR function within NHS organisations. A diverse range of HR practices was reported as being involved, and how the practices operated varied by organisation. HR managers complained of overwhelming workloads, of not feeling that their role was understood, and of having to manage conflicting priorities. The HR function was described as being involved in a number of areas which were raised as concerns in the consultations:

- recruitment and retention

- training and development

- pay and rewards

- communication

- teamworking.

Recruitment and retention

There was a reported turnover of around 20 per cent of new starters in some NHS organisations, in addition to significant proportions of staff close to retirement. This meant that recruitment was a priority for many participants, not only those from the NHS:

We have an ageing workforce and in a few years will not have enough staff.
(Private sector HR director)

Recruitment and retention was an issue for HR managers and clinical managers, and tensions emerged between these staff groups about how to work closely together to improve recruitment and retention.

There was a view expressed in the consultation that co-ordination and ownership of induction processes between the HR function and the work area concerned was needed and not always present.

There was little evidence of co-ordinated attempts to retain newly recruited staff as pressures to pursue recruitment dominated, although HR managers recognised a need to manage candidates' expectations prior to recruitment to tackle the high turnover of new recruits. Competition for employees was differentiated locally: competitors for support staff represented a range of local organisations, such as supermarkets, and competitors for clinical staff represented local and national NHS providers as well as private and charitable health care providers.

Participants in the consultation suggested that the HR function should develop knowledge about why people leave, and develop strategies to address these problems.

NHS organisations have been involved in international recruitment drives and identified additional training needs to successfully integrate new international staff. Overseas recruitment resulted in significant cultural challenges in the wider team. Work was required to manage the implications and results of international recruitment and to meet specific staff training needs.

Concerns were raised about some of the technical aspects of recruitment which were outside the control of the organisation but impacted on speed of recruitment, not only for staff from overseas. Criminal records and home office checks were specifically mentioned as slowing the process down.

The NHS was recognised as a good employer with favourable terms and conditions. However, participants suggested that the NHS had a poor public image as an employer. Linked to recruitment and retention is the issue of removing staff – something that was described as very problematic. The NHS is seen as an employer offering considerable employment security:

It's hard to get rid of staff, especially with the sick pay benefits. Also, it's heavily unionised and no one takes responsibility for dealing with problem staff.

(HR manager)

Staff turnover may not necessarily provide an effective measurement of commitment because staff cannot always go anywhere else – eg a local Trust may have a monopoly over the nursing community.

We should think about staff choice, not just patient choice – and recognise the demands of the NHS workforce.

Some concerns were expressed about the quality of transactional HR in organisations – the quality of job descriptions, the panel and how it performs at interview, the quality of contracts, the occupational health experience – despite recognition that this is not an issue in all organisations.

Training and development

Training and development initiatives included the introduction of appraisals and personal development planning, and discussion revolved around how effectively and extensively they were being introduced.

We never used to have appraisals in the NHS, so how they fit is, therefore, unknown.

(HR manager)

A key issue is access to appraisals and personal development programmes and how we develop values that people recognise, like supporting and understanding performance indicators.

(HR director)

I find it very shocking that there are no appraisal systems, especially for non-clinicians. The NHS could communicate values, identity and cohesiveness and promote a direction towards one goal this way.

(HR manager)

Participants in the consultation suggested that the HR function should make sure appraisals happen – be custodian but not 'take over' the issues, keeping the responsibility with the staff member.

Training and development strategies were aimed mainly at clinical staff, historically, but this was changing as a result of recruitment and retention strategies and with role redesign initiatives aimed at developing skills of existing staff groups. Some difficulties were experienced when private companies provided staff for the NHS but did not provide training. Training and development needs were said to be not always linked to organisational needs and goals.

'... there was a clear understanding of the limitations on permissible rewards within the NHS that divided public and private sector participants.'

Pay and rewards

Pay and rewards were discussed at some length, not least because of the imminent introduction of the national pay spine (for all staff apart from doctors) through *Agenda for Change*. However, there was a clear understanding of the limitations on permissible rewards within the NHS that divided public and private sector participants.

It was suggested that many leavers cited dissatisfaction with pay as their reason for leaving. They also described work intensification with no related increases in pay. Banding systems for pay were proving problematic at the time of the consultation meetings as staff expectations often exceeded their rating. Inclusion of staff in job-matching increased the understanding of the banding system. Job-matching was also illustrating current inequalities in holiday allowances between, for example, admin staff and nurses. This standardisation of the pay system dominated the time of HR managers as deadlines for introduction of the pay spine fell in late 2005.

In contrast, clinical staff suggested that pay was not as important as being able to feel they made a difference. Pay was described as a hygiene factor, not something that made a huge difference to performance.

It was considered important for staff to gain recognition for having done good work. However, there was also considerable resistance from NHS participants to differential reward systems for individuals. Those who work in high-performing areas are currently provided the same benefits/extras as those working in poorly-performing areas.

There were said to be no financial rewards for discretionary effort, and no respect or recognition for additional effort either. This was said to decrease discretionary effort generally as there was a lack of give-and-take between managers and staff. There were conflicting views about discretionary effort in the NHS. Some staff groups were described as having a '9 to 5' culture. Debate centred on whether this was a culture problem or a result of lack of recognition of discretionary effort. There was also some concern that *Agenda for Change* may not allow for the reward and recognition of good work.

Private sector participants described the pay and reward structure as archaic. Examples were given from the hospitality industry where star performers were singled out for rewards. Those participants from the NHS were in favour of recognition at a team level rather than for specific individuals.

The means of providing public recognition for good work was variable amongst Trusts, each deciding the kinds of rewards it used. An example was given of working in the NHS for 25 years and receiving a 'certificate' following the suggestion (from another participant) that rewards are not matched to achievements. Other examples included awards given in the ambulance service sponsored by suppliers where achievements could be celebrated. There were accounts of celebratory events for organisational successes. Additional systems were organised through the HR function – eg employee of the month. Celebrations were found to be acceptable to NHS employees because they did not represent big cash prizes but were able to offer recognition of effort. Recognition events could be used to capture the changes required to achieve organisational performance.

Communication

The need for effective communication was linked to understanding of a bigger picture (wider organisational and NHS goals) and to engagement with organisational aims and values. Although information was cascading down the system, it was more problematic to feed information up into the system.

NHS patient satisfaction surveys provided key information about communication in the organisation and suggest that communication is a major problem. These surveys provide information back for staff and may be used to structure training and development.

NHS organisations obtain Trust-level information on staff satisfaction through the annual staff survey, but this information is not always sent back to the front line employees.

You have to talk to staff before changing and implementing things. This is very important … It's common sense, but we lost it somewhere.

(Clinical manager)

A PCT case study

HR staff are used as 'performance coaches' as well as having a member on the senior team and Board. From Board level down, the PCT has focused on what behaviours the Trust wants to portray – ie dignity/respect – and addressed what is meant by these behaviours. They have developed 'champions', and an approach including 'background conversations'. [Background conversations: a means of surfacing barriers to effective communication and trust. Barriers are reduced without adversely impacting dignity and respect.] HR have created a 'vision' and filtered it out to the organisation. All members of staff attended a day trip to discuss vision, values and background conversations. Staff are encouraged to get opinions out in the open. This scheme has been running now for three to four years, and is being maintained. The system is now used to introduce innovation, whereas it was originally used to help with disputes. It resulted in the decrease in grievances to zero, and employees can request 'background' committed conversations with 'counsellors'. HR helps others to actually listen and find that results in performance pay off for the organisation.

Teamworking

Teamworking discussions revolved around management relationships, particularly relationships with direct managers.

Team leaders were identified as managers of change and were said to need training to help in this role.

We need to try to encourage employees in simple ways to make similar elements of their job easier. Rather than extra paperwork we could find simpler ways of recording. If we could show how this relates to performance targets and financial impact, that would help.

(HR manager)

'Some conflict stemmed from the exclusion of doctors and senior managers from the national pay spine.'

We need to get integrated teams. Thinking about the patient and how they are affected gets people talking and listening. This can result in job redesign and change teamworking.

(Clinical manager)

The impact of national policy initiatives

National Health policy sets the direction for human resource management at a national and local Trust level and was a prominent part of the consultation discussions. Policies impacting on daily HR practice included:

◘ *Agenda for Change* – aimed at pay reform and workforce modernisation and linked to the knowledge and skills framework

◘ the Working Time Directive – instituting European regulations and impacting on working hours; it will affect recruitment and retention

◘ the National Programme for IT – linked to electronic staff and patient records

◘ *Improving Working Lives* – good employment practice.

Participants identified the local difficulties and opportunities they were encountering when attempting to implement HR-related aspects of health policies. Difficulties arose for two reasons: either through competing contradictory policies – ie between those applying to health and those applying to social care – or through conflicts between national policy and specific local conditions. The two national policies discussed at length were *Agenda for Change* and *Improving Working Lives*.

Where the HR functions seem to be focused on interpreting policy, consultation participants suggested the creation of cross-disciplinary work groups to develop the local implementation of these policies.

Agenda for Change

Many of the participants were involved in preparing for the implementation of the national pay spine *(Agenda for Change)* and were currently undertaking job evaluations and job-matching activities. The policy was described as a 'one-size-fits-all agenda for pay'.

Some participants found their time completely taken up with these activities and felt unable to tackle the workforce modernisation agenda linked to the initiative. Indeed, they felt that they lacked the necessary expertise to effect workforce modernisation. This was not the case for all participants and there were others who had been able to prepare for implementation with little difficulty. The difference seemed to lie in how staff had been engaged in the process and pre-existing levels of trust between staff and managers. In addition, the Knowledge and Skills Framework was either used as a checklist in the evaluation process or as a creative tool for forward planning.

Some participants in the consultation felt that the rate of change can be slow. Particular reference was made to the 'long' time it has taken to implement *Agenda for Change*.

There were some reservations about the effectiveness of this approach. Some conflict stemmed from the exclusion of doctors and senior managers from the national pay spine. Some participants were concerned that although pay may be maintained, staff may feel a loss of status as the total number of grades is reduced.

Agenda for Change aims to modernise, but I'm not sure it equals rewards and recognition. The banding system for pay is problematic. You can move up a band, but then you have to apply for a job to get on to the next band. Plus there are problems with different holidays/time off, etc, between admin staff and nurses, yet are all going to be put on the same band. It's all part of the idea to standardise the system.

(Clinical manager)

There is some local autonomy over pay with Agenda for Change, but with current implementations, 'matching' pay is unlikely to occur. Generally, I don't believe that the new system can be sustained – ie trying to change what is currently 70 pay spines into 8! Grading and status is a major issue for NHS staff. Changing the pay spines can be demotivating regardless of pay remaining the same because with limited spines you can't work up the system.

(HR director)

Trust directors were particularly concerned about the financial implications of the new pay spine and of potential responses to individual reductions in pay resulting from standardised overtime payments.

Currently, we are balancing our books, but if we implement Agenda for Change, suddenly we could be £16–20 million over budget.

(Trust director)

If you work on weekends or nights, then you would get a percentage added onto your pay. Potentially people's wages are going to drop – ie if you are paid time-and-a-half rather than double-time for bank holidays.

(Clinical director)

It was also suggested that it would take some time to realise benefits such as performance improvements from *Agenda for Change*.

There is more emphasis on balancing pay than on performance.

*

Agenda for Change has forced Trusts to work in partnership with employees. It will be 12 months before we see any real benefits from Agenda for Change.

*

Some people find role redesign threatening. I think it encourages them to think for themselves and raises the question 'How can we achieve it?' Agenda for Change came along to encourage people to examine what they are doing and to decide what needs to be done. It focuses on service delivery.

Accounts of implementation ranged from feeling consumed by the *Agenda for Change* 'monster' to enjoying the challenge across the organisation. In some cases preparation for implementation was causing staff to find out about what happened in the wider organisation, increasing relationships, improving staff involvement and encouraging interactions.

HR capacity was absorbed in preparing for *Agenda for Change* in some organisations.

The size of it is the main problem – we keep reminding ourselves that it will be worth it in the end.

Agenda for Change was also having an impact on the private health sector as staff working in the private sector demand similar working conditions to those in the NHS.

Ambulance Trust

Ambulance Trusts face specific challenges and have their own targets – specifically around speed of response to emergency calls. Ambulance Trusts are different from Acute Trusts, but are now an integrated part of the NHS and are very clear on their focus and on delivering health care. Previously, HR had an advisory position. Now they are involved in collaboration and partnership with employees. There is very limited contracted-out work except for cleaning and re-kitting of ambulances for the next shift. The organisation employs very few agency employees, only agency clerical staff. Agency ('bank') staff come from other ambulance services. This Trust is able to offer overtime to its own staff working to fill gaps. *Agenda for Change* will increase salaries, but decrease overtime. Fixed rotas result in less flexibility for staff but they can allow employees to predict, in the long term, when and where they will be working. This Ambulance Trust recognised specific organisational challenges and was able to identify a changing approach to HRM.

Improving Working Lives

Improving Working Lives (IWL) was mentioned as an additional concern, although little was said about how it was being implemented. Most Trusts met their performance target. This was at least partly because of the immediacy of the *Agenda for Change* deadlines. Some participants felt that their employers paid lip service to the IWL initiative rather than actively seeking involvement. It was also discussed in connection with difficulties in achieving work–life balance for those implementing *Agenda for Change*, for example.

Electronic staff record

It was hoped that the introduction of the electronic staff record would ameliorate some procedural aspects of the HR function by unifying staff records across organisations. In addition, there were hopes that this record would enable an organisation to maximise its use and knowledge of staff skills – eg provide a record of staff language skills for the purposes of interpretation.

The implications of new policy implementation

There were several suggestions made by participants relating to or arising from policy initiatives detailed below:

- to increase capacity for workforce modernisation and role redesign

- to be clearer about possibilities for local flexibility to match national goals with local needs (centralised process – things constantly coming down)

- to improve the links between policies to reduce conflict and ensure parity; to use pilot studies where there is chance to evaluate before rolling out a programme.

HR within individual organisations

The consultation showed that participants believed that there was a wider role for HR than simply supporting the transactional elements of HR within the organisation, which is in line with changes in

HRM as a whole and its potential contribution to adding value to the organisation. This is reflected in the views expressed about the definitions of terms (see pages 11–13) but also in other comments about aspects of the organisation.

Structure, strategy and capacity

Among NHS participants, several structural arrangements for the provision of HR were identified, which ranged from HR representation at Board level to external contracting for HR services to other NHS Trusts. Where organisations had a HR director, they were better able to recount effects of the integration of the HR function at organisational level – ie inclusion and contribution to wider strategic decision-making about workforce planning or service developments.

There was a view from some organisations that they simply had insufficient capacity within the HR function to fulfil what was expected of them both locally and in response to national initiatives – something described as an 'overwhelming workload'. It was suggested that individuals should set realistic expectations and HR should view their role as offering advice to managers and staff, rather than doing so many things for them.

There was a recognition that a strategic approach to HRM was needed and that HRM had to be integrated with strategic objectives if it was to influence performance.

Do we have a Trust HR strategy that is clear about the Trust's responsibility, the impact of people management, etc, that is brought to life? Does it have CEO involvement? Is the strategy related to front line managers?

Acute Trust

This Trust uses a business partnership approach to managing the organisation. Plans for a new hospital on the existing site are under way – however, sources of new employees have not been found. The Trust initiated a scheme for competency development through a pilot linked with KSF. The organisation won an award for redesigning roles. The organisation recognises the need to get people together and talking, but they are often engrossed in doing other things – ie targets, finance – and the people element therefore gets forgotten. Where do HR and people come in the hierarchy? It was unclear whether the Board recognised HR issues without a HR director, and so people management issues are overlooked.

HR relationships with line managers

As HR practitioners have moved away from traditional personnel management, they have come into conflict with line managers who seem to still require the support they have been used to. This formed a source of conflict, as HR managers suggested that line managers shy away from responsibility for managing their staff and line managers feel they lack the expertise to deal with issues such as recruitment and disciplinary matters.

In contrast, some HR staff felt that they were not consulted enough by line managers who 'did what they wanted anyway'. There was considerable emphasis on improving the relationships between HR and line managers, and suggestions ranged from offering more training to having dedicated local staff working closely together to share expertise and expectations.

Participants suggested that in some cases there was a lack of clarity about HR function and HR issues were not understood. This could be addressed by a variety of means:

◘ holding events that explore people management issues – perhaps a big event

◘ HR as a function raising its visibility – having a proactive presence

◘ the HR function might go out to staff, rather than waiting for them to come to it

◘ ensuring that HR staff learn about the business – especially the clinical side

◘ raising the profile of the role of HR at staff induction.

The following quotes provide examples of opposing viewpoints:

They [line managers] expect HR to do their dirty work, so if you have a problem you get sent to personnel.
(HR manager)

I don't have time to take care of absence, turnover, grievances, etc, and anyway, we don't have the expertise to manage this.
(Clinical manager)

The relationship between line managers and human resource managers was a key determinant of effective people management. This theme emerged at each meeting and formed a focus for debate between HR and non-HR participants. There was a division of opinion whereby HR managers recognised a lack of capacity and capability of line managers in some aspects of people management. In contrast, line managers did not want to make a mistake and wished to draw on expert advice.

For example, when dealing with the sickness and absence of a staff member, HR managers argue that this is a local management problem whereas line managers want to draw on expert advice from HR specialists. Further sources of conflict included debate about responsibility for issues such as disciplinary action and recruitment. HR were said to have expert knowledge that was sometimes difficult to access and line managers did not have the expertise to deal with certain people management processes.

HR professionals stated that they were often called in late on disciplinary matters, and felt that it would be helpful to be involved earlier. They recognised the need for pastoral support as well as visible and individual relationships between named HR staff and managers and staff.

The focus of these debates were relational – ie on how HR managers and line managers worked together to achieve their goals.

Some HR professionals who took part in the consultations recognised that the attitude of the HR function might have to change if working together was to be effective. HR must engender greater flexibility to allow managers to be creative – eg focus on how to pay 'unusual shift' employees rather than saying it cannot be done.

It was suggested that decentralisation of the HR function would improve relationships and shared understanding. Additionally, increased face-to-face contact and/or more extensive training, tools, and support for line managers could resolve many of these conflicts.

Participants suggested that as well as individual appraisal, staff could observe services and comment, somewhat like a peer-review process

By recognising the desire of line managers to avoid making mistakes, HR managers suggested coaching systems whereby line managers would administer processes under expert guidance and processes would move towards line managers and away from HR. These processes included recruitment and disciplinary measures. Such an arrangement would also enable HR managers to understand the specific needs of certain departments.

One participant raised the issue of the restricted ability of the HR function to manage individuals effectively, especially with regard to short-term sickness. Perhaps this is something that needs to be delegated effectively to line managers.

One organisation had set up service-level agreements between HR and specific departments, recognising that the customers of HR in the NHS are the staff, not the patients. This arrangement set expectations about what HR could achieve, clarified responsibilities between HR and managers, and addressed tensions as line managers were clear about what was expected of them.

A private mental health care provider (PHC)

HR operates as a traditional personnel function in this organisation. 'We are left in the dark.' There are no communication mechanisms in place between HR staff, each unit having a different HR manager and no involvement of HR in organisational decision-making. The HR manager had attempted to put processes in place so that staff could express grievances and suggested that staff did not feel allowed to speak out or have opinions. The majority of people management problems resulted in formal grievances and absences. There is a lack of communication between managers and staff and no HR initiatives to improve this. The organisation is managed reactively with little opportunity for staff involvement. Policies are implemented without consulting staff. The approach to communication is dissemination of information top-down, with no channels to hear back from staff. Very occasionally there are staff forums. The organisation has no union recognition. Staff leave because of poor working conditions and poor pay and conditions, especially holidays. There is a lack of co-ordination between units in the company and a lack of pay harmonisation because individuals negotiate their pay on arrival.

'The inclusion of HR measures in the performance measurement system was felt to have recognised the contribution of human resource management to overall organisational performance.'

The HR role in service design

Participants recognised that the HR function was often not involved in service design, even when there were workforce implications. Whereas some participants simply suggested that HR should 'get involved' with service and workforce planning, others recognised the challenge and proposed that HR should be more flexible to fit people into new roles

The HR contribution to organisational culture

Some participants in the consultation suggested that the HR function should be looking to facilitate 'organisational development, not organisational maintenance'.

Other participants felt that the HR function had an important role to play in creating a non-punitive culture within the organisation. In a climate of change, managing the integration of a number of cultures, and the associated number of different expectations of HR, was a key challenge.

The challenges of HR when working in partnership with other organisations

There were other challenges identified as being associated with organisations working in partnership, although most of these related to the transactional elements of the HR function.

Difficulties working across boundaries were reported – especially health and social care. One organisation was implementing *Agenda for Change* but another had single-status employment conditions. It was suggested that there should be more effective recognition of HR issues – eg disparity in pay, terms and conditions, regulatory differences.

New organisational forms were identified as raising challenges in managing teams where there are mixed cultures/processes/regulations.

Linking HRM and performance

The NHS brings together a range of organisations to provide health care and, therefore, patient care outputs are measured differently for each organisational type. Comparisons are possible across similar trust types – ie Acute Trusts, Ambulance Trusts, Mental Health Trusts and Primary Care Trusts. There are common measures for staff satisfaction across all trusts.

The inclusion of HR measures such as *Improving Working Lives* in the performance measurement (star rating) system was felt to have recognised the contribution of human resource management to overall organisational performance. The Knowledge and Skills Framework and complaints systems were said to contribute to understanding of links between HRM and performance.

HRM was viewed as having more impact on performance when it was tied into other things – eg change management, with involvement for example in NPfIT.

There was considerable interest in being able to link HRM and performance outcomes, particularly those outcomes relating to patient care – for example, treating people with dignity and respect. The delivery of high-quality patient care was a common shared value of those who took part in the consultation meetings – not only clinical staff but also managers and directors.

Participants felt that staff are loyal to patients, their profession and their team, but often not loyal to the organisation (Trust). This was perceived as impacting on what HRM can achieve – and it was felt that it would be more effective if it could be more clearly linked to patient outcomes – ie showing that it 'made a difference'.

6 | Conclusion and implications

Key messages

◘ The NHS is the largest employer in Europe: a complex organisation, undergoing significant structural change, where the impact of market forces is increasingly being felt.

◘ Those who work to provide health care, not all of whom are employed by the NHS, cover a wide range of types of work, and are from a variety of professional groups.

◘ Formal performance management from a national perspective is relatively new within the NHS and the national framework for its assessment has changed substantially from 2005 onwards. The nature of the performance measures used in the NHS is very different from other types of organisation.

◘ There is insufficient evidence to suggest that any one HR practice is superior to another in terms of its effect on performance.

◘ There is little agreement, either in theory or in practice, about the role of HRM in organisations, how the HR function might be resourced and organised.

◘ The HRM–performance link is shown to be complex and multi-factorial, with little evidence of a causal link between HRM and performance.

◘ While the NHS is clearly different from other types of organisation, this does not imply that a new theory of the relationship between HRM and performance is needed, rather that great care is needed when utilising approaches or practices that have not already been applied in this context.

◘ The nature of the link between HRM and performance relationship (i.e. the "how" and "why") is not clearly elaborated in the literature.

This chapter draws together conclusions and implications for the NHS and identifies areas for further research. Although this Report does not contain detail of empirical research, there are a number of key implications for the NHS. The next phase of this study is also described here.

The NHS

There are a number of characteristics of the NHS which make it different from other types of organisation, both in the private and public sectors.

'The ... market economy within the NHS offers great potential for the transfer of policies and practices ... shown to be effective in other sectors'

It is the largest employer in Europe

The size and scale of the NHS means that any central initiative will take considerable time and resources to implement throughout the organisation – something illustrated by the introduction of *Agenda for Change*.

Perceptions from those working locally are that pressure to implement central initiatives leaves little, if any, resource for locally-developed initiatives. There is also inevitable variation in scope and quality of local HRM capability, as well as capacity. However, the positive aspects of a large organisation should not be forgotten: the potential for learning and sharing of best practice is vast.

Implications:
The NHS needs to both

- capitalise on its size by ensuring that good practice is shared, and

- remember that size means that implementation of central initiatives will take time and may benefit from local flexibility.

The organisational structure is complex and changing

The relationship between the Department of Health and the local organisations in terms of both policy and practice is complex, not least because of market changes. The NHS consists of a wide range of organisation types, with primary care currently undergoing further reorganisation and the introduction of Foundation Trusts affecting all sectors. These changes also affect the balance of central and local responsibility, with plans to devolve more decision-making from the centre to local organisations.

Implications:
Changes to responsibility and structure mean that a 'one-size-fits-all' approach to management, and to HRM, is less likely to be either appropriate or achievable. This also affects models of 'best practice'. Local organisations must be able to balance

- the need for some central approaches to HR – eg employee relations, performance-related pay – with

- local freedoms, especially as market forces have more of an effect.

It operates in a partial market

Compared to private sector organisations, where market forces are the key drivers for strategic development, the NHS operates in a partial market, so that the full impact of market forces is not experienced. This has always been the case in the NHS, but policy developments which seek to increase the impact of market forces within the UK health sector are likely to have even more impact in future. This may give more freedom to develop local strategies and approaches to HRM, but will continue be influenced by the role played by the professionals in these new types of organisation.

Implications:
The continued development of a market economy within the NHS offers great potential for the transfer of policies and practices which have been shown to be effective in other sectors. However, there will be limits, not only because the market is partial but also because of the legacy of the public sector ethos for many staff which will affect implementation of any new policy or practice.

'There is debate about whether there is a clear "vision" for the NHS ... '

Health care is delivered by a range of staff, not all employed directly by the NHS

The trend towards contracting out of elements of service provision means that those delivering the service may not have a direct 'line management' responsibility to the NHS, being employed by other organisations. The exact numbers of staff in this position is not known, but the trend is towards more staff delivering health care who are not directly employed by the NHS.

Implications:

The impact of NHS HR policies will be affected by the proportion of staff involved in delivering health care but not employed by the NHS. Recent proposals for the organisation of primary care mean that many primary care services may be delivered by those employed by organisations other than the NHS. Commitment to the NHS cannot be assumed from all those providing services, especially where they are not directly employed. However, it should not be assumed that such staff will not be committed to the values of the NHS.

Those delivering health care are 'professionals'

The number and range of professionals employed within the NHS has implications for the nature of 'line management'. Staff share loyalty to patients, their profession and their team, but not always to their organisation or employer. The history of management in the NHS has also left a legacy of confrontation rather than co-operation in some cases. It was suggested that this impacted on what HRM can achieve. A closer link to patient outcomes was thought to be desirable – ie showing that HRM 'made a difference'.

The introduction of a new performance framework (Department of Health, 2005j) which places more emphasis on support for those in professional roles may help to address this issue.

Implications:

The need to support the professional 'instincts' of NHS staff is acknowledged in policy documents but not always apparent in practice, where both the 'system' and 'management' are at times perceived to be in conflict with professional interests. Managers at a local level must be careful to ensure that the initiatives they utilise, and the way they implement them,

make it easier for dedicated doctors and nurses ... to follow their calling to cure and to care.

(Department of Health, 2002)

The purpose of the NHS

There is often a gap between the stated purpose of the NHS and the reality as perceived by those who work within it. There is debate about whether there is a clear 'vision' for the NHS, although recent policy developments have emphasised a patient-centred NHS. Those participating in the consultations appear to have a common shared value – that of improving patient care.

Implications:

In order to make the transfer of approaches accomplished in the private sector, it would be helpful for the NHS to have a clear statement of purpose articulated which relates to the strategy being employed and which can be used to focus effort across all professional groups and organisations. It should not be assumed that all staff share the same objective when change is being introduced.

'There is opposition to the process of performance management from some staff ... '

HRM

HRM in organisations

There are a variety of perspectives on HRM from a theoretical standpoint. However, in practice, HRM varied and did not conform easily to any of the main theoretical perspectives.

Implications:
The promotion of any element of HRM should be undertaken with regard to the context in which it is being introduced. Care should be taken in adopting practices from other sectors given the many differences between the NHS and other types of organisation.

HRM in the NHS

From a national perspective there have been considerable changes in the way HRM is administered, such as the establishment of NHS Employers, which reduced the role of the DH. Changes in the size and composition of the workforce are likely to continue as markets are opened up. Recent proposals for changes to primary care organisations (Department of Health, 2005k) mean that potentially all primary care could be provided by non-NHS organisations by 2008.

Implications:
The HR function at a local level does not necessarily have responsibility for all staff involved in delivering the service, and although there is local awareness of this, national recognition of the implications is less clear.

HR as a function

The direction of the HR function and activity in NHS organisations is driven primarily by national policy – eg *Agenda for Change*. There is no common structure for the HR function or a common pattern of reporting at a strategic level within NHS organisations.

Implications:
The HR function at a local level does not currently appear to have sufficient capacity to influence all the 'people management' aspects of the local organisation, and although there is some resourcing of HR development, the size of the NHS means that this is slow to impact. Locally, recognition of the limitations and current capabilities of the HR function require recognition, and nationally flexibility towards approaches is required.

Elements of HRM

Key authors do not agree about the optimal 'bundle' of HR practices that should be employed by organisations. The empirical evidence suggests that 'practices' may in reality also be policies, strategies and systems – terms are not used in a precise way. Because of the divergence of evidence, it is more appropriate to emphasise 'good' rather than 'best' practice.

Implications:
There is no evidence to suggest that a single element of HRM will have a dramatic effect on performance; it may therefore be advisable to focus on identifying and spreading 'good' rather than 'best' practice, recognising the benefits of a diversity of approaches.

Performance

Performance management

There is no explicit link between NHS strategy and the performance framework used, although both are broadly focused around the improvement of patient care. There is opposition to the process of performance management from some staff, and debate about the most appropriate performance measures, even where the process is accepted. This makes it difficult for key objectives to be linked to performance criteria. Performance measures themselves are numerous and complex.

Implications:
Although the link between strategy (and the policies which follow from it) and performance could always be more clearly articulated, this is a complex issue. Locally, staff may not understand why they are required to do and measure certain things.

Performance assessment and measures

Detailed performance information for the NHS up to April 2005 (derived from the star rating system) is publicly available. However, this performance management framework had relatively little focus on HR. There is a new performance framework for the NHS with more focus on the staff contribution to performance. A range of measures are used but few focus on individual patient outcomes.

Theoretical studies concerned with HRM and performance have tended to over-emphasise financial measures of performance, so there is little guidance from theory to support such new developments.

Implications:
Although the new performance framework appears to be an improvement on the previous one, careful monitoring from the start at both a national and local level is required to ensure that the contribution of HRM is given appropriate emphasis.

Performance measures currently used within the NHS may differ from those used in previous studies, which have largely focused on the private sector and a range of industries. In addition, the NHS is positioned within a largely centrally-driven and political arena, and structural changes will affect performance.

HRM and performance

The HRM–performance link

The link between elements of HRM and the HRM–performance relationship (ie *how* and *why* HRM affects performance) is not clearly elaborated in the literature. The HRM–performance link is shown to be complex and multi-factorial, with little evidence of a direct causal link between HRM and performance.

There are methodological limitations in existing studies – even where studies attempted to investigate the causal relationship. Most empirical information has been drawn from single-respondent surveys. Empirical evidence comes from a wide range of industries. There is little research at the present time within the health sector.

Implications:
Monitoring of the implementation of any new element of HRM should be done using appropriate methodology, taking into account the complexities

'There is very little about *how* or *why* HRM is linked to performance ...'

of the practice and its relationship to other practices. The context of the implementation of any element of HRM is important and should be taken into account.

Mediators of the HRM–performance link (the 'black box')

There are a number of perspectives on the relationship between HRM and performance, which include resource-based, psychological, sociological and economic theories. However, the literature does not clearly differentiate these perspectives. In general, the mediators of the HRM–performance relationship have not been investigated or tested rigorously. There is very little about *how* or *why* HRM is linked to performance, although research has considered discretionary effort, commitment, the impact of the psychological contract and the influence of managers and/or culture.

Implications:
It is possible that the key factor determining the effect of HRM on performance is the impact on the individual; the wide range of studies carried out so far have not often explored this in detail.

The next phase of the study

Phase one of this study outlined existing evidence linking HRM and performance and investigated policy implications for NHS employees. A detailed consultation process gave information about HRM and performance on the ground.

The next phase of the study will address the following questions:

- ◘ how HR processes, practices and polices affect performance

- ◘ how HR processes, practices and policies combine/interact to meet organisational needs/goals

- ◘ what are the constraints and enabling factors for effective HRM, including context

- ◘ how tailoring of HR practices might best be achieved and delivered in NHS settings.

These questions concern *how* and *why* HRM contributes to achieving organisational goals.

Six in-depth case study sites will be conducted including 'high performance' and 'transformational' sites, and will include two Acute Trusts, two PCTs and two mental health Trusts. These sites will be selected from those who have been either consistently high performers over the last three years (using star rating data) or those who have transformed their performance over that period by at least two stars. At each site staff will be sampled from four categories – professionals, support staff, staff working in partnership and those contracted from other organisations to provide services. A cross-section of staff will be taken from all levels of the organisations. This will give insight into how individual attitudes and behaviours influence performance at individual, group and organisational levels.

⌈ **'The study of HRM within health care is going to continue to be important in the coming years '**

Future research possibilities

It is clear from current policy developments within the NHS that the study of HRM within health care is going to continue to be important in the coming years. The work reported here shows that health and social care staff have values and attitudes, motivations and resultant behaviours that may be distinct from those in the private sector. There is scope for further investigation concerning successful human resource management in the health and social care sector.

This could be achieved through a series of reviews focused specifically on certain areas such as managing staff across organisational boundaries, multiple sites and with varied contractual arrangements, including within the health and social care sector, HRM within new organisational forms, such as network organisations which are being adopted increasingly within the NHS, and mediators of the HRM–performance relationship which may be specific to health and social care. Such reviews would also support existing research on organisational forms within the NHS – eg that commissioned by the NHS Service Delivery and Organisation Programme (www.sdo.lshtm.ac.uk).

The role of PCTs is changing with the increased use of contracting, changes in commissioning, partnership working and networks of larger organisations. What are the implications of working across these organisational boundaries to deliver effective services?

Mental health and social care Trusts bring together health and social care organisations. How will the differing backgrounds and cultures of these organisations affect the delivery of care and the way in which HRM should be practised?

Primary research is useful where there are new or emerging empirical phenomena which need further exploration. A programme of research bringing together academics from a variety of backgrounds may enable creative exploration of these areas.

The introduction of Foundation Hospitals gives the opportunity for more local adaptation of national policies and the development of local policies. How will this occur in practice?

Increasing numbers of providers in health care, especially in the secondary care sector, will affect staff working together across organisational boundaries. What challenges does this raise from the perspective of HRM?

Appendix 1

Limitations of the literature review

The scope of the review

Research described only in reports (eg the Sears reports), books and chapters has not been included (eg Appelbaum *et al*, 2000). The decision to include only peer-reviewed academic journals is in line with best practice, and provides a mechanism for 'quality control' of the papers analysed. However, some studies may have been missed as a result.

The use of three databases restricts the papers included to those in journals indexed by those databases. However, a further search for key authors was conducted, so the main papers do seem to have been located.

Studies which focused on the validation of selection and assessment procedures, CEO pay or pay modelling were not included. Expert advice indicated that these would be substantial systematic reviews alone.

Papers which only included an HRM outcome such as absence and turnover, or on any specific health outcomes, were not included because the focus of the review was on organisational-level performance outcomes.

Publication bias may mean that editors prefer to publish papers that report significant associations, and this would lead this review to over-estimate the strength of association between HRM and performance.

Papers published before 1994 were not included, following expert advice and in line with other reviews (Wall and Wood, 2005). The HRM

paradigm shift from 'personnel' to HRM took place just before this date and so most papers from 1994 onwards would reflect HRM.

The process of review

There may be some degree of human error in including papers and extracting papers, despite the use of more than one reviewer at most stages of the process.

The use of any inclusion criteria means that some papers will not be included that might be in other similar reviews because of variance in criteria (eg see Boselie *et al*, 2005).

The analysis of the papers

Analysing in terms of elements of HRM is complex because:

◘ some studies have focused on individual practices/policies, and others on multiple practices/policies. Bunching (for example) 'training' together fails to account for the type of training that is being measured in each study and how it was implemented.

◘ Some studies have focused on the detail of elements of HRM while others have focused simply on whether the element is present or not.

Analysing papers together using performance measures is complex because different measures have been used for different levels of analysis (organisational, team, individual, customer).

The method of analysis used in the studies varies considerably, so drawing conclusions about the strength of associations is difficult.

◨ Some studies reported here rely on correlations and descriptive data.

◨ Others use regression, and analysis of variance, path analysis, etc.

Research designs vary – although the papers in this review are predominantly cross-sectional surveys. Within this, however, there are differences about how HRM and performance has been measured and the respondents used – which limits generalisability.

Appendix 2

Glossary

'Black box'	Describes the factors that mediate the link between HRM and performance
Best fit	Otherwise known as 'contingency' – one of the theoretical perspectives on the HRM–performance relationship, which proposes that to experience competitive advantage, HR practices need to be aligned with business strategy
Best practice	Otherwise known as 'high commitment' – one of the theoretical perspectives on the HRM–performance relationship, which proposes that there are a set of HR practices which will give the best impact on performance
Care Trusts	Care Trusts may carry out social care, mental health services or primary care services and are set up when the NHS and Local Authorities agree to work closely together
Department of Health (DH)	The Department's role is to help improve the health and well-being of the population of England. It provides strategic leadership to the NHS and social care organisations in England and has overall responsibility for:

■ setting the direction of health and social care services in England

■ setting and monitoring standards for health and social care services

■ ensuring NHS and social care organisations have the resources they need

■ ensuring patients and the public can make choices about the health and social care services they use.

Empirical literature	Academic papers which contain the results of research carried out on 'real' organisations, as opposed to theoretical content
Employee	An individual working within, and employed under an employment contract, by the organisation.
Foundation Trusts	Foundation Trusts are a new type of NHS hospital run by local managers, staff and members of the public which are tailored to the needs of the local population
High-performance paradigm	The overall concept of the relationship between HRM and organisational performance

HR practices	Set of practices used to manage the workforce of an organisation – ie recruitment, selection, training, involvement – usually promoted by the HR function
	The term 'elements of HRM' is also used to refer to these practices
Human Resource Management (HRM)	In general, the management of people within the organisation, *not* a specific function. This includes consideration of the management of people at a strategic level within the organisation
Human Resources (HR)	The HR function/department within the organisation. Whereas 'human resources' are employees, personnel, or the workforce of an organisation, the term is used here to refer to an organisational function. Sometimes the term "HR" is used interchangeably with 'HRM' by staff within organisations.
Mental Health Trusts	Specialist mental health care is normally provided by Mental Health Trusts, often in partnership with other organisations
NHS	The National Health Service in England
NHS Trusts	Hospitals are managed by NHS Trusts (also known as Acute Trusts)
People Management	All aspects of how people are managed by line managers. It is a broader activity than that carried out by the HR function
Primary Care Trusts (PCTs)	PCTs are organisations responsible for commissioning and managing health services in a local area. They may also provide some services themselves
Resource based view (RBV)	One of the theoretical perspectives on the HRM–performance relationship, which focuses on the internal resources at the disposal of the employer, rather than treating factors external to the organisation as the main drivers of HRM
Strategic Health Authorities (SHAs)	SHAs develop plans for improving health services in their local area, make sure local health services are of a high quality and are performing well, and make sure that national priorities are integrated into local health service plans

References

AIKEN, L., SMITH, H. and LAKE, E. (1994)

'Lower Medicare mortality among a set of hospitals known for good nursing care', *Medical Care*, 32:771–787.

ALLISON, G. (1979)

Public and private management: are they fundamentally alike in all unimportant respects? in *Classics of Public Administration* (Eds, Shafritz, J and Hyde, A) Belmont.

ANON (2005)

So what do the experts say? *The Guardian*, London, p.16.

APPELBAUM, E., BAILEY, T., BERG, P. and KALLEBERG, A. L. (2000)

Manufacturing advantage; The Effects of High Performance Work Systems on Plant Performance and Company Outcome. Ithaca, NY: Cornell University Press.

APPLEBY, J. and DEVLIN, N. (2005)

Measuring NHS success. London.

APPLEBY, J., DEVLIN, N., HARRISON, A. and DEEMING, C. (2002)

A critical appraisal of NHS systems of performance measurement, London

APPLEBY, J., HARRISON, A. and DEVLIN, N. (2003)

What is the real cost of patient choice? London.

APPLEBY, J. and MULLIGAN, J-A. (2000)

How well is the NHS performing? London.

ARAH, O. A., KLAZINGA, N. S., DELNOIJ, D. M. J., ASBROEK, A. H. A. T. and CUSTERS, T. (2003)

'Conceptual frameworks for health systems performance: a quest for effectiveness, quality, and improvement', *Int J Qual Health Care*, 15:5 377–398.

ARTHUR, J. B. (1994)

'Effects of human resource systems on manufacturing performance and turnover', *Academy of Management Journal*, 37:670–687.

BACKOFF, R. W. and NUTT, P. C. (1992)

Strategic Management of Public and Third Sector Organisations: A Handbook for Leaders: San Francisco, Jossey-Bass.

BACON, N. and BLYTON, P. (2005)

'Worker responses to teamworking: exploring employee attributions of managerial motives', *International Journal of Human Resource Management*, 16:2 238.

BAILEY, T. (1993)

'Organizational innovation in the apparel industry', *Industrial Relations*, 32:30–48.

BARNEY, J. (1991)

'Firm resources and sustained competitive advantage', *Journal of Management*, 17:1 99–120.

BARNEY, J. (1995)

'Looking inside for competitive advantage', *Academy of Management Executive*, 9:4 49–61.

BENKHOFF, B. (1997)

'A test of the HRM model: good for employers and employees', *Human Resource Management Journal*, 7:4 44.

BLYTON, P. and TURNBULL, P. (2004)

Dynamics of Employee Relations 3rd Edition. London: MacMillan Press.

BORRILL, C., WEST, M., SHAPIRO, D. and REES, A. (2000)

'Team working and effectiveness in health care', *British Journal of Health Care*, 6:364–371.

BOSELIE, P., DIETZ, G. and BOON, C. (2005)

'Commonalities and contradictions in HRM and performance research', *Human Resource Management Journal*, 15:3 67–94.

BOSELIE, P., PAAUWE, J. and RICHARSON, R. (2003)

'Human resource management institutionalisation and organisational performance: a comparison of hospital, hotels and local government.' *International Journal of Human Resource Management*, 14:8 1407–1429.

BOURNE, M., MILLS, J., WILCOX, M., NEELY, A. and PLATTS, K. (2000)

'Designing, implementing and updating performance measurement systems', *International Journal of Operations and Production Management*, 20:7 754–771.

BOXALL, P. (1996)

'The strategies HRM debate and the resource-based view of the firm', *Human Resource Management Journal*, 6:3 59–75.

BOXALL, P. and PURCELL, J. (2003)

Strategy and Human Resource Management. Houndmills: Palgrave/Macmillan.

BOYNE, G. A. (1996)

'The intellectual crisis in British public administration: is public management the problem or the solution?' *Public Administration*, 74:679–694.

BRADLEY, J. R. and CARTWRIGHT, S. (2002)

'Social support, job stress, health and job satisfaction among nurses in the United Kingdom', *International Journal of Stress Management*, 9:3 163–182.

BUCHAN, J. (2004)

'What difference does ('good') HRM make?' *Human Resources for Health*, 2:6 online only.

CAPPELLI, P. and NEUMARK, D. (2001)

'Do 'high-performance' work practices improve establishment-level outcomes?' *Industrial & Labor Relations Review*, 54:4 737–770.

CAULKIN, S. (2003)

People and public services: why central targets miss the mark. London: CIPD.

CHAN, Y-C., LILIAN (2004)

'Performance measurement and adoption of balanced scorecards: a survey of municipal governments in the USA and Canada', *International Journal of Public Sector Management*, 17:3 204–221.

CHANG, P. C. and CHEN, W. L. (2002)

The effect of human resource management practices on firm performance: Empirical evidence from high-tech firms in Taiwan, *International Journal Human Resource Management*, 19(4): 622.

COFF, R. (1997)

'Human assets and management dilemmas: coping with hazards on the road to resource-based theory', *Academy of Management Review*, 22:2 374–402.

CROMBIE, I. K. and DAVIES, H. T. O. (1998)

'Beyond health outcomes: the advantages of measuring process', *Journal of Evaluation in Clinical Practice*, 4:1 31–38.

CROSS, K. F. and LYNCH, R. L. (1988/9)

'The SMART way to define and sustain success', *National Productivity Review*, 9:1.

CULLY, M., WOODLAND, S., O'REILLY, A. and DIX, G. (1999)

Britain at Work: As depicted by the 1998 Workplace Employee Relations Survey. London: Routledge.

CUNNINGHAM, L. AND HYMAN, J. (1999)

'Devolving HR responsibilities to the line – beginning of the end or a new beginning for personnel?' *Personnel Review*, 28:1–2 9–27.

CURRIE, G. (1999)

'The influence of Middle Managers in the business planning process', *British Journal of Industrial Relations*, 10:2.

CURRIE, G. and PROCTER, S. (2001)

'Exploring the relationship between HR and middle managers', *Human Resource Management Journal*, 11:3 53–69.

DASH, P. (2004)

'New providers in UK health care', *BMJ*, 328:7435 340–342.

DELANEY, J. T. and HUSELID, M. A. (1996)

'The impact of human resource management practices on perceptions of organizational performance', *Academy of Management Journal*, 39:4 949–969.

DELANEY,J. T., LEVIN D. and ICHNIOWSKI C. (1989)

Human resource policies and practices in American firms; Washington DC: US Government Printing Press.

DELERY, J. E. and DOTY, D. H. (1996)

'Modes of theorising in strategic Human Resource Management: tests of universalistic, contingency and configuration performance predictors', *Academic of Management Journal*, 39:4 802–835.

DELERY, J. E., GUPTA, N., and SHAW, J. D. (1997)

Human Resource Management and firm performance: a systems perspective

DEPARTMENT OF HEALTH (2000)

The NHS Plan: a plan for action, a plan for reform, London.

DEPARTMENT OF HEALTH (2002)

HR in the NHS Plan – more staff working differently, London.

DEPARTMENT OF HEALTH (2004a)

Staff in the NHS 2004: An overview of staff numbers in the NHS

http://www.dh.gov.uk/PublicationsAndStatistics/Statistics/ StatisticalWorkAreas/StatisticalWorkforce/fs/en
Accessed 20 June 2005

DEPARTMENT OF HEALTH (2004b)

About the Department

http://www.dh.gov.uk/AboutUs/HowDHWorks/DHWorkArticle/fs/
en?CONTENT_ID=4106148&chk=fq4zcZ
Accessed 20 June 2005

DEPARTMENT OF HEALTH (2004c)

*The NHS Improvement Plan: Putting people at the heart of public
services,* London.

DEPARTMENT OF HEALTH (2004d)

Chief Executive's report to the NHS, London.

DEPARTMENT OF HEALTH (2004e)

*Standards for Better Health: Health Care Standards for Services under
the NHS,* London.

DEPARTMENT OF HEALTH (2005a)

Speech by Rt Hon Patricia Hewitt MP, Secretary of State for Health,
17 June 2005: Speech to NHS Confederation conference

http://www.dh.gov.uk/NewsHome/Speeches/SpeechesList/
SpeechesArticle/fs/en?CONTENT_ID=4113723&chk=eYKAdf
Accessed 29 Jun 2005

DEPARTMENT OF HEALTH (2005b)

*A workforce response to local delivery plans: a challenge for NHS
boards,* London.

DEPARTMENT OF HEALTH (2005c)

HR Capacity Unit

http://www.dh.gov.uk/PolicyAndGuidance/
HumanResourcesAndTraining/BuildingPeopleManagementSkills/
HRCapacityUnit/fs/en?CONTENT_ID=4051432&chk=hn3IXz Accessed
9 Sep 2005

DEPARTMENT OF HEALTH (2005d)

Creating a Patient-led NHS: delivering the NHS Improvement Plan,
London.

DEPARTMENT OF HEALTH (2005e)

The NHS Plan

http://www.dh.gov.uk/PolicyAndGuidance/OrganisationPolicy/
Modernisation/NHSPlan/fs/en?CONTENT_ID=4082690&chk=/DU1UD
Accessed 29 Jun 2005

DEPARTMENT OF HEALTH (2005f)

Delivering the NHS Improvement Plan: the workforce contribution,
London.

DEPARTMENT OF HEALTH (2005g)

Productive Time Programme

http://www.dh.gov.uk/PolicyAndGuidance/
HumanResourcesAndTraining/ProductiveTime/
ProductiveTimeProgramme/fs/en
Accessed 21 Jun 2005

DEPARTMENT OF HEALTH (2005h)

Speech by Sir Nigel Crisp, Chief Executive, to the NHS Confederation
Conference, 16 June 2005

http://www.dh.gov.uk/NewsHome/Speeches/SpeechesList/
SpeechesArticle/fs/en?CONTENT_ID=4113717&chk=W%2BVz6p
Accessed 29 Jun 2005

DEPARTMENT OF HEALTH (2005i)

Speech by Rt Hon Patricia Hewitt MP, Secretary of State for Health,
13 May 2005: Speech to HR in the NHS Conference

http://www.dh.gov.uk/NewsHome/Speeches/SpeechesList/
SpeechesArticle/fs/en?CONTENT_ID=4110963&chk=HNsfJI
Accessed 29 Jun 2005

DEPARTMENT OF HEALTH (2005j)

*National Standards, Local Action: Health and Social Care Standards
and Planning Framework 2005/06–2007/08,* London.

DEPARTMENT OF HEALTH (2005k)

Commissioning a patient-led NHS, London.

DEVANNA, M. A., FOMBRUN, C.. and TICHY, N. (1984)

A framework for Strategic Human Resource Management, New
York: Wiley.

DOUCOULIAGOS, C. 1995.

'Worker participation and productivity in labor-managed and
participatory capitalist firms: A meta-analysis'. *International and
Labour Relations Review*, 49(1): 58.

DRIFE, J. and JOHNSON, I. (1995)

*Handling the conflicting cultures in the NHS in Management for
Doctors* (Eds, Simpson, J. and Smith, R.), London, BMJ Publishing.

EDWARDS, P. K. (1986)

Conflict at Work: A Materialist Analysis of Workplace Relations.
Oxford: Blackwell.

ESKILDSEN, J. K., KRISTENSEN, K. and JUHL, H. J. (2004)

'Private versus public sector excellence', *The TQM Magazine*, 16:1
50–56.

FITZGERALD, L., JOHNSTON, R., BRIGNALL, T. J. and SILVESTRO, R. (1991)

Performance Measurement in Service Businesses, London.

GAKOVIC, A. and TETRICK, L. E. (2003)

'Psychological contract breach as a source of strain for employees', *Journal of Business and Psychology*, 18:2 235–246.

GELADE, G. A. and IVERY, M. (2003)

'The impact of human resource management and work climate on organisational performance', *Personnel Psychology*, 56(2): 383–404.

GERSHON, P. (2004)

'Releasing resources to the front line', *Independent Review of Public Sector Efficiency,* London.

GLYNN, J. J. and MURPHY, M. P. (1996)

'Failing accountabilities and failing performance review', *International Journal of Public Sector Management*, 9:5/6 125–137.

GODARD, J. (2004)

'A critical assessment of the high performance paradigm', *British Journal of Industrial Relations*, 42:2 349.

GODDARD, M., MANNION, R. and SMITH, P. C. (1999)

'Assessing the performance of NHS Hospital Trusts: the role of 'hard' and 'soft' information', *Health Policy*, 48:119–134.

GOULD-WILLIAMS, J. (2003)

'Importance of HR practices and work place trust in achieving superior performance: A study of public sector organisations', *International Journal Human Resource Management*, 14(1): 28–54.

GREENER, I. (2005)

'Health Management as Strategic Behaviour', *Public Management Review*, 7:1 95–110.

GUEST, D. (1987)

'Human Resource Management and Industrial Relations', *Journal of Management Studies*, 24:5 503–21.

GUEST, D. (1997)

'Human resource management and performance: a review and research agenda', *International Journal of Human Resource Management*, 8:3 263–76.

GUEST, D. (1999)

'Human resource management: the workers' verdict', *Human Resource Management Journal*, 9:3 5–25.

GUEST, D., MICHIE, J., SHEEHAN, M., CONWAY, M. and MATOCHI, M. (2000)

Employment Relations, HRM and Business Performance. London: CIPD.

GUEST, D. M. J., CONWAY, N. and SHEENAN, M. (2003)

'Human Resource Management and corporate performance in the UK', *British Journal Of Industrial Relations*, 41:2 291–314.

HARLEY, B., HYMAN, J. and THOMPSON, P. (2005)

Participation and democracy at work: Essays in honour of Harvie Ramsay. Basingstoke: Palgrave Macmillan.

THE HEALTHCARE COMMISSION (2005a)

What is the Healthcare Commission and why we exist?

http://www.chai.org.uk/AboutUs/WhatIsTheHealthcareCommission/WhatIs/fs/en?CONTENT_ID=4000066&chk=jP1mlc
Accessed 21 Jun 2005

THE HEALTHCARE COMMISSION (2005b)

The annual health check: what you need to know

http://www.healthcarecommission.org.uk/InformationForServiceProviders/AnnualHealthCheck/fs/en?CONTENT_ID=4017483&chk=ub2qrx
Accessed 21 Jun 2005

THE HEALTHCARE COMMISSION (2005c)

Assessment for improvement:Criteria for assessing core standards. London.

HEBSON, G., GRIMSHAW, D. and MARCHINGTON, M. (2003)

'PPPs and the changing public sector ethos: case-study evidence from the health and local authority sectors', *Work, Employment and Society*, 17:3 483–503.

HOPE-HAILEY, V., GRATTON, L., MCGOVERN, P., STILES, P. and TRUSS, T. (1997)

'A chameleon function? HRM in the 1990's', *Human Resource Management Journal*, 7:3 5–18.

HOQUE, K. (1999)

'Human resource management and performance in the UK hotel industry', *British Journal of Industrial Relations*, 37:419–443.

HUSELID, M. A. (1995)

'The impact of human resource management practices on turnover, productivity and corporate financial performance', *Academic of Management Journal*, 38:3 635–72.

HUTCHINSON, S. and WOOD, S. (1995)

The UK experience, Personnel and the line: Developing the new relationship. IPD: London.

ICHNIOWSKI, C., SHAW, K. and PRENNUSHI, G. (1997)

'The effect of human resource management practices on productivity: A study of steel finishing lines', *American Economic Review*, 87(3): 291.

KAPLAN, R. S. and NORTON, D. P. (1992)

'The balanced scorecard: measures that drive performance', *Harvard Business Review*, 70:1.

KEEGAN, D., EILER, R. and JONES, C. (1989)

'Are your Performance Measures Obsolete?' *Management Accounting*, 70:12 45–50.

KENNERLEY, M. and NEELY, A. (2002)

'A framework of the factors affecting the evolution of performance measurement systems', *International Journal of Operations and Production Management*, 22:11 1222–1245.

LAKHANI, A., COLES, J., EAYRES, D., SPENCE, C. and RACHET, B. (2005)

'Creative use of existing clinical and health outcomes data to assess NHS performance in England: Part 1--performance indicators closely linked to clinical care', *BMJ*, 330:7505 1426–1431.

LANE, J. (1993)

The Public Sector. Sage, London.

LEACH D. J., WALL T. D., ROGELBERG S. G. and JACKSON P. R. (2005)

'Team autonomy, performance and member job strain: uncovering the teamwork USA link, *Applied Psychology*,. 54(1) 1–24.

LEATHERMAN, S. and SUTHERLAND, K. (2003)

The quest for quality in the NHS: a mid-term evaluation of the 10-year quality agenda. London.

LEES, S. (1997)

'HRM and the legitimacy market', *International Journal of Human Resource Management*, 8:3 226–243.

LEGGE, K. (1989)

'Information technology: personnel managements lost opportunity?' *Personnel Review*, 18:5 2–62.

LEGGE, K. (1995)

Human Resource Management: Rhetorics and Realities. Basingstoke: Macmillan.

LEPAK, D. and SNELL, S. (1999)

'The human resource architecture: Towards a theory of human capital allocation and development', *Academy of Management Executive*, 24:1 31.

LUPTON, B. (2000)

'Pouring the coffees at interviews? Personnel's role in the selection of Doctors', *Personnel Review*, 29:1 48.

MACDUFFIE, J. P. (1995)

'Human Resource bundles and manufacturing performance: organisational logic and flexible production systems in the World Auto industry.' *Industrial and Labour Relations Review*, 48:197–221.

MANNION, R. and DAVIES, H. T. O. (2002)

'Reporting health care performance: learning from the past, prospects for the future', *Journal of Evaluation in Clinical Practice*, 8:2 215–228.

MANNION, R., DAVIES, H. T. O. and MARSHALL, M. N. (2005)

Cultures for performance in health care. Maidenhead Open University Press.

MARCHINGTON, M., GRIMSHAW, D., RUBERY, J. and WILLMOTT, H. (2004)

Fragmenting work: Blurring organisational boundaries and disordering hierarchies. Oxford: Oxford University Press.

MARCHINGTON, M. and WILKINSON, A. (2000)

Direct Participation. London: Blackwell.

MARCHINGTON, M. and WILKINSON, A. (2005)

HRM at work: People, Management and Development. CIPD: London.

MCADAM, R. and CROWE, J. (2004)

'Assessing the business and employee benefits resulting from the implementation of NVQs', *Education & Training*, 46:2/3 138–152.

MCGOVERN, P., GRATTON, L., HOPE-HAILEY, V., STILES, P. and TRUSS, C. (1997)

'Human Resource Management on the line?' *Human Resource Management Journal*, 7:4 12–29.

MEIKLE, J. (2005)

Quality's the new measure The Guardian London, pp. 2–3.

MICHIE, J. AND SHEEHAN-QUINN, M. (2001)

'Labour market flexibility, human resource management and corporate performance', *British Journal of Management*, 12:4 287–306.

MILES, R. AND SNOW, C. (1984)

'Designing strategic Human Resource Systems', *Organizational Dynamics*, Summer:36–52.

MORGAN, G. (2005)

Comment The Guardian, London, p.4.

MORIARTY, P. and KENNEDY, D. (2002)

'Performance measurement in public sector services: problems and potential' *Performance Management Association Conference, Centre of Business Performance*, Boston

MORRISON, E. W. and ROBINSON, S. L. (1997)

'When employees feel betrayed: a model of how psychological violation develops', *Academy of Management Review*, 22:1 226–257.

MOULLIN, M. (2002)

Delivering Excellence in Health and Social Care. Buckingham Open University Press.

MURRAY, B. and GERHART, B. (1998)

'An empirical analysis of a skill-based pay programme and plant performance outcomes', *Academy of Management Journal*, 41(1): 68.

NEELY, A. (1999)

'The performance measurement revolution: why now and what next?' *International Journal of Operations & Production Management*, 19:2 205–228.

NEELY, A. D., ADAMS, C. and KENNERLEY, M. (2002)

The Performance Prism: The Scorecard for Measuring and Managing Stakeholder Relationships. London, FT/Prentice Hall.

NUTLEY, S. and SMITH, P. C. (1998)

'League tables for performance improvement in health care', *Journal of Health Services Research and Policy*, 3:1 50–57.

OSBORNE, S. P., BOVAIRD, T., MARTIN, S., TRICKER, M. and WATERSTON, P. (1995)

'Performance management and accountability in complex public programmes', *Financial Accountability and Management*, 11:1 19–37.

PARK, H., MITUSHASHI, H., FEY, C. and BJORKMAN, I. (2003)

'The effect of human resource management practices on Japanese MNC subsidiary performance: A practical mediating model', *International Journal Human Resource Management*, 14(8): 1391–1406.

PARKER, R. and SUBRAMANIAM, V. (1964)

'Public and private administration', *International Review of Administrative Sciences*, 354–366.

PASS, S. E. (2004)

Looking inside the 'black box': Employee opinions of HRM/HPWS and organisational performance. Cardiff Business School: University of Wales.

PATTERSON, M., WEST, M. A., LAWTHORNE, R. and NISKELL, S. (1997)

Impact of people management practices on business performance. London: Institute of Personnel and Development.

PENROSE, E. (1959)

The Theory of the Growth of the Firm. Oxford: Blackwell.

PFEFFER, J. (1994)

Competitive Advantage through people. Boston: Harvard Business School Press.

PFEFFER, J. (1998)

The Human Equation: Building profits by Putting People first. Boston: Harvard Business School Press.

PIL, F. and MACDUFFIE, P. (1996)

'The adoption of high involvement work practices', *Industrial Relations*, 35:421–455.

POLLOCK, A. M., SHAOUL, J. and VICKERS, N. (2002)

'Private finance and 'value for money' in NHS hospitals: a policy in search of a rationale?' *BMJ*, 324:7347 1205–1209.

PORTER, M. (1985)

Competitive Advantage: Creating and Sustaining Superior Performance. New York: Free Press.

PURCELL, J. (1999)

'Best Practice and best fit:chimera or cul-de-sac?' *Human Resource Management Journal*, 9:3 26–41.

PURCELL, J., KINNIE, N., HUTCHINSON, S., RAYTON, B. and SWART, J. (2003)

Understanding the people and performance link: Unlocking the black box. London: CIPD.

PURVIS, L. J. and CROPLEY, M. (2003)

'The pscyhological contracts of National Health Service nurses', *Journal of Nursing Management*, 11:107–120.

RADNOR, Z. and MCGUIRE, M. (2004)

'Performance management in the public sector: fact or fiction?' *International Journal of Productivity and Performance Management*, 53:3 245–260.

RAMSAY, H., SCHOLARIOS, D. and HARLEY, B. (2000)

'Employees and high-performance work systems: Testing inside the black box', *British Journal of Industrial Relations*, 38:4 501–531.

RANSON, S. and STEWART, J. (1994)

Management for the Public Domain. London.

RUBERY, J., EARNSHAW, J., MARCHINGTON, M., COOKE, F. L. and VINCENT, S. (2002)

'Changing organisational forms and the employment relationship', *Journal of Management Studies*, 39:5 645–672.

SAYRE, W. (1953)

'Premises of public administration', *Public Administration Review*, 18:102–103.

SCHULER, R. S. and JACKSON, S. (1987)

'Linking competitive strategies and Human Resource Management practices', *Academy of Management Executive*, 1:3 207–219.

SHAW, C. (2003)

How can hospital performance be measured and monitored? Copenhagen.

SHEAFF, R., SCHOFIELD, J., MANNION, R., DOWLING, B., MARSHALL, M. and MCNALLY, R. (2004)

Organisational factors and performance: A review of the literature.

SIDDIQUE, C. M. (2004)

Job analysis a strategic human resource management practice, *International Journal of Human Resource Management*, 15(1): 219–244.

SISSON, K. and STOREY, J. (2000)

Realities of human resource management: Managing the employment relationship. Buckingham: Open University Press.

SMITH, P. C. (2002)

'Performance management in British health care: Will it deliver?' *Health Affairs*, 21:3 103–112.

SMITH, R. (2003)

'Is the NHS getting better or worse?' *BMJ*, 327:7426 1239–1241.

SPARROW, P. R. and COOPER, C. L. (2003)

The employment relationship: Key challenges for HR. Oxford Butterworth-Heinemann,.

SVYANTEK, D. J., GOODMAN, S. A., BENZ, L. L. and GARD, J. A. (1999)

'The Relationship Between Organizational Characteristics and Team Building Success', *Journal of Business and Psychology*, 14:2 265–283.

THOMSON, R. (2002)

Process or outcome measures for quality improvement and performance management of health care providers: a discussion paper. Newcastle Upon Tyne.

TICHY, N. M., FOMBRUN, C. J. and DEVANNA, M. A. (1982)

'Strategic human resource management', *Sloan Management Review*, 23:2 47–61.

TORRINGTON, D., and HALL, L. (1998)

Human Resource Management, 4th Edition. Hertfordshire: Prentice Hall.

TRUSS, C. (2001)

'Complexities and controversies in linking HRM with organizational outcomes', *The Journal of Management Studies*, 38:8 1121–1149.

ULRICH, D. (1997)

'Measuring human resources: an overview of practice and a prescription for results', *Human Resource Management Journal*, 36:3 303–515.

VERE, D. and BEATON, L. (2003)

Delivering public services: engaging and energising people. London.

WALL, T. D. and WOOD, S. J. (2005)

'The romance of human resource management and business performance, and the case for big science', *Human Relations*, 58:4 429–462.

WEST, M., BORRILL, C., DAWSON, J., SCULLY, J., CARTER, M., ANELAY, S., PATTERSON, M. and WARING, J. (2002)

'The link between the management of employees and patient mortality in acute hospitals', *International Journal of Human Resource Management*, 13:8 1299–1310.

WHITTAKER, S. and MARCHINGTON, M. (2003)

'Devolving HR responsibility to the line: Treat, opportunity or partnership?' *Employment Relations*, 25:3 245–261.

WISNIEWSKI, M. and STEWART, D. (2004)

'Performance measurement for stakeholders', *International Journal of Public Sector Management*, 17:3 222–233.

WOOD, S., and ALBANESE, M. (1995)

'Can we speak of a high commitment management on the shop floor?' *Journal of Management Studies*, 32:2 215–247.

WOOD, S. and DEMENEZES, L. (1998)

'High Commitment Management in the UK: evidence from the Workplace Industrial Relations Survey and Employers' Manpower and Skills Survey', *Human Relations*, 51:4 485–515.

WRIGHT, P. and GARDNER, T. (2003)

'The human resource-firm performance relationship: Methodological and theoretical challenges' in *The new workplace: A guide to the impact of modern working practices*. (Eds, Holman, D., Wall, T., Clegg, C., Sparrow, P. and A, H.). John Wiley & Sons Ltd.

WRIGHT, P., MCMAHAN, G. and MCWILLAMS, A. (1994)

'Human Resources and Sustained Competitive Advantage: A resource-based perspective', *International Journal of Human Resource Management*, 5:2 301–26.

YOUNDT, M. A., SNELL, S. A., DEAN, J. W., JR. and LEPAK, D. P. (1996)

'Human resource management, manufacturing strategy, and firm performance', *Academy of Management Journal*, 39:4 836–866.